two weeks with the Psychic Surgeons

by MARTI SLADEK

Published By: DOMA PRESS / P.O. BOX 1995 / CHICAGO, ILLINOIS 60690

Photo credits: Don Sladek, Marti Sladek

Published by:

Doma Press
P.O. Box 1995
Chicago, Illinois 60690
U.S.A.

Library of Congress Catalogue Number: 76-45732
ISBN 0-917816-01-3

With love to my husband, Don.

We have used real names in this book except in a few cases where it was desirable to protect people's privacy.

ACKNOWLEDGEMENTS

You cannot include in a dedication all the people who contribute to a book such as this; there are too many, whose aid is too varied and ideas too numerous to mention. But we would like to express our appreciation to some of the people who have helped to guide us along the path we are now taking, and whose selflessness has given us courage at times when we had doubts and fears:

Brad Steiger—whose assistance and encouragement made it all possible.

Joe and Alexandria East—psychic and graphologist respectively, who head "The Group" in Chicago.

Deon Frey—psychic, mentor and good friend.

Harold Schroeppel—founder, Institute for Advanced Perception, Oak Park, Illinois.

Lasca Bogdanove—yogi, professor, astrologer.

Mr. and Mrs. Floro Cruz—examples of the warmth and sincerity of the Filipino people.

Louise and John Hyland, Brent Ferre and others who shared their own Philippine experiences with us.

Virginia Watkins—our film editor and friend.

Jack Gorham—naprapath and, more importantly, crusader.

Eleanore Gorham—who was kind enough to donate her time to help with the proofreading.

John Difino and his very professional staff at Graphic Services Corp.

Tony Sladek—for moral support.

We are deeply indebted to the following people who took time out from hectic schedules to contribute material for this book simply because they share our commitment: Stanley Krippner, George Meek, Hans Naegeli, John Newcombe, Lee Pulos, Harry Rich, Henry Rucker, and Sigrun Seutemann.

CONTENTS

FOREWORD

In the entire area of paranormal research today, there is perhaps no greater maelstrom of controversy than that which swirls about psychic surgery. Although I believe that we must be open-minded in our approach toward dramatic demonstrations of ostensible abilities currently beyond the ken of our sciences, I am compelled to state that we must also view these same occurrences with caution and common sense. Regrettably, there is no single area of human endeavor which breeds more charlatans and ghouls than that which purports to minister to the physical suffering of men and women.

If it is possible that certain individuals can channel Love Energy to the extent that they can literally part human flesh with a mere gesture, remove invading organisms or diseased organs with their bare hands, then instantly rejoin the penetrated body without leaving mark or scar, nearly all of our established precepts of what constitutes material reality must run limping for cover.

In the light of the reality construct suggested by psychic surgery, our most sophisticated medical machinery becomes but technological excuses for the manifestation of the true healing energies which lie dormant within every man and woman on the planet.

If the psychic surgeons really are doing what they claim, then everyone of *us,* as well as our orthodox physicians, have the innate ability to heal ourselves.

But should the psychic surgeons be merely sleight-of-hand performers (either self-deluded or greed-motivated), then the person whose body has yielded to the human condition of physical illness would be well-advised not to yield further to the ministrations of charlatans—regardless of how sincere or well-meaning they may appear to the untutored eyes of laymen.

I, frankly, am on the fence in regard to psychic surgery. I know that the true healing force is really quite aloof from bromides or nostrums. I accept the reality of what is loosely termed "faith healing," for I have witnessed many fine healers at work. But I also call upon the orthodox medical artisans on occasion when either myself or my family needs a little help from our friends.

I have a friend, an open-minded professional magician, who states that he has caught the very best of the psychic surgeons employing trickery.

I have another friend, an open-minded physician, who reports that his analysis of the tissue removed by a psychic surgeon tested out to be of sheep, rather than human, origin. Yet this same doctor attested that in a number of cases the patients' tumors and so forth had somehow "dematerialized" from their bodies. We might then conjecture that palmed bogus tissue and butchershop blood served as physical stimuli which, coupled with the patients' belief, triggered their bodies' own healing mechanisms and inspired them to eliminate the invading cells.

And then I have my friends Marti and Don Sladek, who went to the Philippines to witness psychic surgery for themselves. I trust Marti and Don not to seek deliberately to con us or to attempt to sell us something in which they themselves do not believe. They offered their own bodies as tests for the psychic surgeons. They returned both inspired and shaken by their experiences. They are convinced that much of what they witnessed was genuine.

The account of the Sladeks' pilgrimage is certainly an interesting one, and I am quite confident that no one will accuse them of lying about the details of their quest. However, it must remain up to the critical faculties of each reader to assess in his own mind whether or not Don and Marti are presenting the truth and the reality of what actually occurred—or whether they are reporting the truth and the reality as they were able to understand it.

Whichever way the reader may vote after he has completed this book, he will surely come away from the text demanding that an authoritative agency with all the proper credentials make an extensive and serious study of the enigma of psychic surgery.

Brad Steiger
November 7, 1975

PROLOGUE

Psychic Surgery is, by its very nature, mind-boggling and controversial. It is the ultimate application of what is called, for lack of a better term, "faith healing." It is painlessly opening and closing the human body without using instruments, anesthesia, drugs, or hypnosis: a phenomenon that means rethinking what we "know" about medicine, physics, biology, psychology, religion, etc.

The uneducated peasants who perform these "miracles" refer to themselves simply as "Healers." Their beliefs are basic to all the great religions, though some of the specific concepts are foreign to most westerners. What these people do may appear to contradict everything we accept as "true." But then, scientific knowledge is constantly changing as new universal laws are discovered, or applications of old ones expanded to new dimensions. The Healers perform "psychic surgery" almost routinely, because no one ever told them it is impossible.

This book is a journal, a diary, of a trip to the Philippines in April, 1973 that changed our lives. I am a reporter by training and experience, but this book is not intended to be objective or quantitative. Where there is documentation available, I have used it. But I have not attempted to prove anything. I've only recorded what happened to us, as we perceive it. I leave it to others to look at the Healers from the objective journalist's or scientist's point of view. I only know what we witnessed, and the things we felt in heart and mind.

For the reader, this book may be neither definitive nor conclusive. It is not intended to be—you may take it any way you wish: to satisfy your curiosity, expand your consciousness, or gather knowledge in preparing to take a trip yourself to see the Healers. For many people, this book may raise as many or more questions than it answers, but that is alright, for that, too, opens the way to progress and deeper understanding. We only ask one thing, and that is not to dismiss the whole thing out of hand without seriously and thoroughly checking into it. There's nothing wrong with skepticism. But refusing to look at something merely because it could pull the rug from under your current system of beliefs is a sin of omission of the first order.

We can't say that other people who go to the Philippines will get the kind of help we did, because every case is different. There are no guarantees. We aren't advising anybody to hop a plane, leave their medication at home and all their problems will be instantly solved. It just doesn't work that way. What we can do is describe our experience, pass on what the Healers told and taught us, and try to counteract some of the misinformation that is circulating about psychic surgery. When we first were researching the Healers, there were only a few books about them, mostly full of case histories and impartial observations. That is necessary. But there is also a place in the literature for a down-to-earth, personalized, subjective account. And this is it.

THE FLIGHT

The last day of March, 1973: a dreary, chilly, overcast, Chicago-style day. Whatever was falling from the sky was suffering an identity crisis—not knowing whether to be rain or snow. We'd have been happy to be going anywhere there was even a hint of real sunshine. As it was, we were in a daze of excitement and anticipation, so leaving that bleak weather was just the icing on the cake. After two years of research and preparation, we were finally going to the Philippines to see the so-called psychic surgeons! We were going to see for ourselves this unique type of "faith" healing, these divinely guided operations performed without pain, drugs, instruments, or scars. I consciously mused on how we'd gotten where we were as I began taking notes, as I always do on a trip.

We don't even remember exactly when we first heard about it. (Like a couple who have been married for decades and don't recall their very first meeting; yet that meeting changed their lives more than any other single event.) In 1970, shortly after we got married, Don took a class in hypnosis—a topic that had interested him for years—from Chicago hypnotist Lee Fitzpatrick. In the course of his experimenting with it, Don used me as the subject for some prenatal regressions and ESP tests; we turned up some startling evidence of both reincarnation and telepathy, though probably not strictly scientific. The details are irrelevant to this particular book, so suffice it to say that we became fascinated with the whole "occult" or whatever you want to call it. We familiarized ourselves with the writings of Brad Steiger, Martin Ebon and Jess Stearn, and read all the Edgar Cayce books, and *Psychic Discoveries Behind the Iron Curtain,* by Lynn Schroeder and Sheila Ostrander. We started attending lectures and psychic fairs, and talking with anyone and everyone we could who was already in the field. We attended meetings of organizations that took vastly different approaches to the subject of the paranormal: The Group, the Illinois Society for Psychic Research, Henry Rucker's Psychic Research Foundation, and the more church-oriented Spiritual Frontiers Fellowship.

At one of the psych-ins, which is a sort of gathering of all kinds of mediums and "fortune tellers," astrologers, spiritualists, and so on, Don was given a reading by David Techter, a well-known psychic. David told him that we would be traveling to a far-off place in the not too distant future, and he saw some islands. He also predicted that Don would be going around the country lecturing professionally. Well, the whole thing sounded pretty ridiculous, as we had not even thought about a long trip; nor did Don have the inclination or expertise to be a lecturer. To compound matters, he was told virtually the same thing by two other psychics over the next few months—Joe East, the head of an occult interest organization known as "The Group," which meets regularly in Chicago; and Harold Schroeppel, who teaches psychic development at the Institute for

Advanced Perception in Oak Park (and whose class we each subsequently took with good results). Actually, Don pushed the whole series of readings out of his mind, far-fetched as they seemed, and didn't even remember them until late in 1973, after we had begun public film showings and lectures on the Philippine Healers!

It was inevitable that somewhere along the line, we would be introduced to the Healers' work and become intrigued. It must have been fall of 1971 when we first saw films of it, underexposed and sketchily narrated at best. But it whetted our curiosity, and every time we heard about a film-showing after that, we tried to go. Some of the films were good, some not so good. Some of the people seemed to know what they were talking about, while others obviously didn't. But there were two people whose presentations impressed us so much that we became determined to make the trip ourselves. Their stories were very convincing.

Brent Ferre, a college student, was born with only one kidney, which was giving out. He'd been taking several kinds of medication, and undergoing dialysis frequently. In addition, he was somewhat hunchbacked. The Ferres had heard about a Healer named Tony Agpaoa, so they took Brent to the Philippines. Tony told them the problem was the spine, that the curvature was putting pressure on the kidney, causing the body to build up a protective layer of tissue around the kidney, which was now threatening to choke the kidney. It was not a conventional medical explanation; nonetheless, Tony said he could fix it.

We saw the films of Brent's operations. Tony did not touch the kidney itself; his hands moved swiftly and surely over Brent's lower back and suddenly the skin seemed to be open. It was very clear on the films. Tony reached into Brent's back and removed the protective webbing from over the kidney. He took away his hand, and as quickly as the opening had appeared, it was gone, leaving no trace or scar. Then he did a magnetic healing, that is, a sort of massage in which healing energy is sent into the body, on Brent's spine, all up and down his back in swirling patterns. He told Brent two things would happen. One, the kidney would begin to regenerate itself (medically impossible) and two, Brent's spine would gradually straighten out and he would grow several inches. Tony advised Brent to take vitamin E and ginseng tea, nothing else. It sounded crazy, but it worked. When we first met Brent a little over a year later, he no longer needed dialysis or drugs, and he was almost two inches taller than he had been before his Philippine trip.

Brent's cure lasted two years, although his spine was still curved. Then he almost died, teaching himself and those he had told about the Healers a valuable lesson. Brent admits the relapse was his own fault, for not taking proper care of himself. He was working, going to school, and showing the films at least once a week. He felt he had an obligation to spread the word—a feeling we certainly empathize with—but he had forgotten his obligation to himself. He nearly undid Tony's work by not using common sense, getting enough rest and/or following a good diet.

It was John and Louise Hyland who began filling in some of the blanks as to how the Healers work. They went to the Philippines for the first time in 1966, when the Healers' work was barely known in the States. It was the Hylands who told us that Tony is not the only Healer; we, like so many Americans, had heard only of him, because he does promote himself a great deal. We knew nothing of the Espiritista, the spiritualist organization most of the other Healers belong to.

John had cancer of the larynx and his voice was nearly gone. He had been taking the controversial drug Krebiozen, which seemed to be helping him, but it was taken off the market; so his only alternative was a laryngectomy, in which the voice box is removed. A bit of information about the Healers had been trickling into the States from Filipino immigrants, U.S. servicemen, etc. John figured he had little to lose and everything to gain by giving it a try. So he and Louise became pioneers in seeking out the Healers in back corners of the Philippines, and disseminating information back home.

John's cancer was cured. The tumor was taken out by a Healer named Ubaldo Corpuz; there was no sign of it when John returned to the States. Corpuz told John that his voice would remain weak for a year or so, but then would come back good as new. That is exactly what happened. Ever since then, John and Louise have been showing films, telling people their experience, and so on, just as Brent was doing and we were to do later on.

We set a tentative date for our own trip several months ahead of time, then shopped around for a reliable travel agent and a reasonably priced tour package, eventually locating a Filipino travel agent in Chicago. He knew about the Healers and, although there were no tours specifically set up for people going to see them, he was able to make special arrangements. Even so, we would need about $3000, which we did not have. (More about that later.) We spent almost all our spare time for four months or so seeing more films, getting as much information as possible, and getting our passports and inoculation records in order. I had traveled some before, so all I had to do was get everything updated and changed to my married name. Don was going through the red tape for the first time: passport application, special photos, and what have you. We both had to get smallpox vaccinations and two cholera shots, as required by the Philippine government. We had everything ready a few days ahead of time as we wanted to take it easy prior to the inevitable last minute rush and the trip—the calm before the storm.

We were to leave on Saturday. The Tuesday before that, we got together with the other members of our tour group and interested friends and relatives to take one more look at the Hylands' films, and clear up last minute questions. Don's folks would be going with us, and also a Nate and Marge Morton, whom we had not met previously but who were hosting the get-together. Don and I were the only ones who were sympathetic to the Healers' religious beliefs in that we, too, are reincarnationists. We had some physical problems we wanted the Healers to work on, but our main purpose in going was to try to tune in on the Healers psychically and spiritually, to see if they are what they purport to be, and if so, how? Nate had an ulcer, and a hernia, and especially wanted to avoid cataract surgery that was already scheduled for the next month. His wife had a long list of physical and nervous disorders. Don's father suffered from a severe heart condition, diabetes, and some related problems; his mother didn't want much done, but was accompanying him mainly for the adventure.

Don's parents almost didn't go. His father had had another heart attack (he'd been hospitalized at least twice a year for the four years I'd known him) just a few weeks earlier. The doctors said the trip would probably kill him, but they had told him he couldn't last much longer anyhow, and that they could not do anything more for him. Actually, he wasn't optimistic about getting help, but felt he deserved a last fling, no matter how slight the hope. United Air Lines had to put him on the plane in a wheelchair for the first leg of the trip, to San Francisco, where we would transfer to Philippine Airlines for the flight to Manila.

I was born into a flying family, and am more at peace in the air than anywhere else, but this was my first time on the Boeing 747. It was a swift, comfortable, fun four hours to the west coast. The time passed quickly as I looked out, imagining myself sitting on the wing; before I knew it, I was looking down at a large, irregular, gray-green patch 30,000 feet below. The Great Salt Lake—as vivid as when we'd stopped to wade there on a trip west the previous summer. Then the thrill of crossing the Rockies. It was strange gazing down at them in all their magnificence, stranger still since on that previous trip we had been looking up at them from the floor of Yosemite valley. I'm really a scenery freak, and my camera was clicking away as if under its own power.

At San Francisco International Airport, we showed our passports to the Filipino officials at the Philippine Airlines desk. They pointed us to the human conveyor belt—a sort of level escalator—that shuttles people across the huge terminal to the gates. Dad was in a wheelchair again. We went through the FAA anti-skyjack check as we had done before boarding at O'Hare. It did not take long, because all we had was our hand luggage, our suitcases having been checked all the way through to Manila at Chicago. At the gate, we took a look at the diverse group of people who'd be our traveling companions for the next 18 hours or so. There was a group of vacationing Americans headed for Australia; most of the other passengers were Filipinos: business people, students, families returning home for the Easter holiday. There was a smattering of Japanese, Chinese, Australians, etc., going to Hawaii, Japan, the Philippines, Hong Kong, and points west and far east. Taking the national carrier of a foreign country you are going to is like getting there early—you meet so many natives, talk to the crew, and get to sample the food even before you set foot on foreign soil!

We were among the first to board, a courtesy extended by the airline since Dad was not at all well. Soon, however, every seat was taken, as the Easter season is one of the busiest times in the Philippines. The plane was a DC-8, large, but not so luxurious as the 747's. At the time, we were under the impression that only Philippine Airlines flies to Manila from the States; not so, as you can get there via various routes on Pan Am, Northwest, and Japan Air Lines, also. But the fact that we were on that particular plane at that particular time was significant. It was the second event of a pattern of "coincidences" which led us by the end of the trip to the conclusion that there is no such thing as coincidence.

The first link in the chain was the way we financed the trip. We had known we would go, come hell or high water, and made our plans accordingly. We had absolutely no idea where we would get that much money. Then, out of the blue, almost on impulse, Don's parents sold their home, and decided to give part of the money to the three sons (not that Don hadn't earned it, working for them without pay for a while several years before). It was exactly the amount we lacked, although up until then, we had not mentioned the trip to them at all. When our prayers were answered, we told them all about it and they started debating whether to come along!

Now, it "just happened" that the only other people on the plane who were going to see the Healers were seated near us, though we did not realize it when we sat down at the very front of the aircraft. Mom and Dad were across the aisle from us, with the Mortons seated immediately behind us. Across the aisle from them, behind Don's parents, sat a young American couple. A 60ish man in a wheelchair occupied the single seat in front of Don's folks. The seats were three across on each side of the aisle. Sharing the right hand section with us was an American man of about 30; he was returning to the Philippines to marry his native fiance, whom he had met while stationed at Cebu Navy Base two years before. A middle-aged Japanese man who runs a travel agency in Honolulu sat with Mom and Dad.

For some reason, the couple behind Don's folks caught my eye. I noticed two things about them: one was that they obviously cared about each other (they weren't particularly demonstrative—there was just something touching in the way they seemed to look to each other for moral support); the second was that they perked up and nudged each other when we began talking about the Healers. They eavesdropped for a short while, then, timidly, the woman asked if we were going to see the Healers, and if so, would we mind sharing any information we had? Of course we wouldn't. By that time, the crippled man, a natural candidate for the Healers, had turned around and joined in, telling us he was on his way to see Tony. We all introduced ourselves. The couple were Mary Ann and Jack Schmidt from Rochester, Minnesota; the man was Joe Bush, a building contractor from Seattle. And suddenly our group had grown from six to nine.

Joe's problem was motor ataxia, a debilitating nerve disease. He was partially crippled all the time and even at his best times had to use a cane. His speech and other brain functions were often impaired and as we later witnessed ourselves, he sometimes lost control of his emotions or memory.

The Schmidts were going on account of Jack, who had been in two serious traffic accidents. His right hip was fused and infected, and he walked with a limp, and head injuries had affected his sight and hearing; he'd been a patient at the Mayo Clinic off and on for 15 years and had had several operations on his hip. Jack and Mary Ann, like us, were just getting into studying mysticism, etc. when they heard about the Healers from a friend who was a medium. We felt they were very brave because, in contrast to our fairly well organized (so far) tour, they were completely on their own. They had Tony's name and address and that was all; they did not know you can't even see him without making an appointment. They had no names or addresses of other Healers, so all in all, were really taking a chance on whether they would get help.

At least, that is what we thought, until we heard why they plunged in with so little preparation: the medium had given them a reading shortly before the trip, at which time she advised them to go ahead.

Everything would be fine, she said, because they would meet another couple who would be able to guide them to the Healers! That sounded pretty incredible to us, and yet here we were, seated right by them on the plane, giving them our list. Actually, it seemed like the proverbial (and in Jack's and my case almost literal) blind leading the blind. But stranger things have happened, and after we heard the tape of their reading a few days later, it was awfully hard to chalk that seating arrangement up to coincidence.

We completely lost track of the time as we got involved in talking about everything in general and the Healers in particular. We had been traveling about 12 hours when we reached our first stop, Honolulu; eight of that had been in the air, four from Chicago to San Francisco and four more from there to Hawaii. Even I was glad to touch terra firma for a while. We were not quite at the halfway point mile-wise, and already we were suffering from jet lag.

Honolulu International Airport is a vision of tropical gardens and tropical moonlight, ocean breezes, fresh air, and flowers. The scent wafts through the entire airport, soothing and almost narcotic. It was a very relaxing 1½ hours, and we never even left the terminal! It was difficult to believe we were still in the U.S., because it seemed more foreign than many places I'd been to in Mexico and Europe. Chicago seemed so far off—if it really existed at all! Don pushed Dad around in the wheelchair so he could enjoy it, too, while I recalled scenes and people from James Michener's *Hawaii* and vowed to spend more time there some day.

We had a snack while they refueled the plane. It was 11:15 at night when we reboarded, once again undergoing the security search. We were beginning to feel the griminess that a long trip does to you. On the plane, we read a little, talked some more, and sort of dozed in that half-awake way you do on a plane, train or bus. Four or five hours out of Honolulu, the pilot announced in his melodic, clipped Filipino accent that because of our exceptionally heavy load (the plane was completely full) and strong headwinds, we would be stopping to refuel at Wake Island. The time changes were getting confusing. By the official clock, it was now 1 a.m., only two hours later than we'd left Hawaii! It would get worse: Manila is 14 hours behind Chicago by the clock, but a full day ahead on the calendar because it is across the International Date Line. I never did figure it out!

Wake Island! It conjured up images of old movies—William Bendix and the Seabees holding out till the last (I know, that was Midway, but the connotation's the same), or John Wayne's boys hoisting the flag on Iwo Jima, not far off as Pacific islands go. It had a certain glorious, albeit treacherous ring. Actually, to the younger ones among us, Wake didn't mean all that much, because World War II doesn't, yet I could feel that almost everyone had the same thought running through their minds as we disembarked. Wake is such a barren spot, the kind of place the phrase "God-forsaken" was coined for; there's just a dingy little USO and some fuel tanks. And everyone was wondering, "For this hole, so many thousands of our boys died?"

Then I happened to glance at the Japanese man, who was walking with Mom and Dad. The irony was too much. He, too, was musing, but to him "our boys" were the Japanese of his generation, and we had been the enemy. Now he owns a business in Hawaii, for the only war we have with our great ally Japan is an industrial one. He caught my eye and smiled wistfully. He knew that I sensed what he was thinking; he was aware that I was thinking it, too.

The vibrations on Wake are incredible. It's a haunted kind of place. The stretch and washup were good but we were terribly glad to get out of there. I was beginning to get bored. Sleep wouldn't come, and I was restless. Out of the window, far below, I spotted a strange light, bright green, but rather like a search beam in its wavering. The stewardess said it was Guam. Guam—another place of war memories and irony. It's very active in contrast to Wake, and on Guam reportedly is located—of all things—the world's largest McDonald's!

Looking down on that light was like looking up at a certain star on a clear night, but topsy-turvy; it seemed close enough to touch, and yet I knew it was so far as to be unreachable. Watching that blinking, emerald speck put me into a kind of reverie. I was fascinated by it, trying to visualize the ground on which it stood. It was extremely dark out. The ocean was some 40,000 feet below through the pitch black; we couldn't see it, but somehow we felt its awesome presence. I kept staring at that light for almost two hours, daydreaming, unable to communicate my feelings to anyone, even Don, until finally, it disappeared under the starboard rudder.

We slept fitfully. Don's father, in great pain, was taking nitro pills like they were M & M's. We were very worried, of course, but neither we nor the crew could do much aside from trying to make him more comfortable. The lights in the plane went on at 5 a.m. Manila time. It was still dark out, because Manila was actually two more hours to the west yet. My little green light had been replaced by a spectacular sight—the first orange rays of the sun behind the airplane, rising, I suppose, at about Guam. It was an odd sensation: we continued to fly into darkness, while breaking light chased us, gradually catching up. I divided my attention between that and a hearty, delicious breakfast.

We began our descent approximately 24 hours after leaving Chicago, though most of the trips don't take that long; we had left Saturday afternoon, yet 24 hours later, it was early Monday morning in Manila. Outside, beyond the wingtips, clouds suddenly merged with ocean, and for the first time, we could see the water on the horizon. Through that misty, sunlit sky, we spotted land below in the form of green-brown rippled soil, rolling away from volcanic peaks. The mountains of the out islands seemed to point up at the plane in greeting as we progressed inland toward the main island of Luzon. I fleetingly thought of the song "Bali Hai" from *South Pacific* (. . . Some day you'll see me, floating in the sunshine, my head sticking out from a low-flying cloud. You'll hear me call you . . .).

It was then, as I frantically began snapping pictures to capture it forever, that it really hit me. We were in the Philippines. We were really going to see the Healers and find out about them and their country firsthand. The combination of excitement and exhaustion was too much. Don felt it, too. He squeezed my hand, and I began to cry.

ARRIVAL

We weren't quite prepared for the blast of hot air that hit us as we got off the plane, because even though it was only 8 a.m. it was already in the 80's. But the humidity was very low, and there was real sunshine, this being the middle of dry season in the Philippines. The weather should have been a welcome relief from Chicago's bleak, long winter; however, we were tired and filthy, and all we could think about was a shower. At the entrance to the terminal, a Filipino girl placed pungent leis of sampaguita around our necks, and the aroma of the country's national flower was overpoweringly sweet.

A travel agency representative prodded us through the document station, where uniformed officials stamped our passports and checked our International Health Cards. Then we claimed our bags—miracle of miracles, they had gotten to Manila at the same time we did, all the way from Chicago! Customs officials shuffled through them half heartedly, as if they were afraid they might find something that would cause trouble for a tourist, but returning Filipinos' luggage was subjected to a much more thorough search.

A young man in a magenta sports coat herded us into a mini-bus, painted the same gauche color, which turned out to be the trademark of the Filipinas hotel, where we would be staying. We were surprised to find so many Filipinos clamoring onto the hotel buses. Later, we found out why: terrorist attacks nearly destroyed the new airport terminal a few years ago, and ever since then, only travelers and authorized personnel have been allowed in the airport. Relatives and friends must wait outside the gates, so people stood along the chain link fence surrounding the airfield, waving and shouting to loved ones and visitors, unable to greet them inside.

The ride to the hotel took about 15 minutes. We couldn't get enough of looking around, trying to drink it all in at once. It was almost enough to make us temporarily forget our sticky discomfort. On one side of the highway was Manila Harbor, filled with military and commercial ships of every description and national registration; on the opposite side was a long strip of hotels and nightclubs, some completed, some under construction. (The Philippines is becoming such a popular tourist spot, they can not keep up with the demand for hotel space and tourist facilities.) We were driving along Roxas Boulevard in the heart of the tourist district, from the airport, past the big hotels, and by the city of Manila's outstanding waterfront parks.

The Philippines is under martial law because of Moslem separatist and communist uprisings on some of the southern islands, although everything is well under control now and a truce has recently been signed. The military was not much in evidence; Philippine martial law was not at all what I expected. It was not openly oppressive, nor were there fierce looking troops everywhere, as I'd seen in East Europe. In fact, the only ones we saw were traffic

M.P.'s and a few guards at government buildings. The connotation of martial law is a bit grim, especially to an American, but in the Philippines, President Marcos' declaration was greeted with enthusiasm in many quarters. We found out why over the course of the trip, observing, and talking to natives. Manila, which used to be a virtual no man's land, is now one of the safest cities in the world. It has also become one of the cleanest, due to a policy of automatically putting polluters and litterers on paint and cleanup details as part of the sentence. And martial law has been a boon to the all-important tourist industry in other ways, for example in protecting foreigners from price gouging. Our travel agent had explained all this before we left, about the positive aspects of the military regime; still, it is very difficult for an American not to consider the civil rights and political aspects!

The Hotel Filipinas was a mob scene, the sidewalks being settings for tearful reunions of Filipinos. We were trying to gather our wits and our suitcases when a young man came up to Don and offered his services as a guide. Don more or less gave him a brush-off, not wanting to deal with that kind of thing yet. We wanted to wash and change into fresh clothes before we even started thinking about anything else! The Mortons and Mom and Dad were going to take it easy for the rest of the day, but we were too keyed up, so we invited the Schmidts, whose hotel was just down the street, to come with us a little later to start checking out the Healers.

Naturally, some suitcases suddenly were missing, one being mine; it had been lost somewhere between the hotel and the airport. Don got cleaned up and went off to track it down. I was miserable. I vowed to myself that next time I would bring a change of clothes in my hand luggage, just in case! We finally located the suitcase in Don's parents' room; a natural error by a bellhop because, after all, her tags also read "M. Sladek." Poor Joe Bush wasn't so fortunate, as his bags didn't turn up until several days later.

I don't know when a shampoo and shower ever felt better to anybody, and if it seems I am obsessed with that in this section, I'm only reflecting our obsession with it then! It took us a while to explore the hotel. We were pleased with what we saw: the Filipinas is sprawling, luxurious, and complete with two dining rooms, shops, swimming pool, beautiful lobby, etc., for about half what you would pay in the U.S. for a modern, air-conditioned hotel.

Jack and Mary Ann Schmidt phoned us about an hour later. They had not been quite so lucky—they'd supposedly had reservations at the Aurelio Hotel, next door to the Filipinas, but they hadn't gone through a travel agent, and in the Philippines, reservations are worthless without one. When they got to the hotel, they were told there were no rooms available. The hotel people did help them find something, though, so they ended up at the Bayview a few doors away. They met us in our lobby and we started out. Don had phoned the first name on John Hyland's list, Professor Tolentino; his wife answered the phone and invited us to come right over.

GOING NATIVE

Jack, Mary Ann, Don and I piled into a cab at the Filipinas. The driver looked a little surprised when we showed him the address; I guess tourists don't ordinarily ask to be taken to a native residential area. And what a cab ride it was! Manila traffic is an incredible mixture of cars, cabs, buses, trucks, jeeps, pedestrians and even horses. The driver spoke little English—just enough to point out some sights, and get a kick out of our jests about his driving. In Manila, only the brave or foolish take a cab at noon rush hour (I prefer to think we were brave). The more we gasped and commented, the faster the driver went, and the more wild, weaving chances he took. Traffic in Paris, Mexico City, and Los Angeles is tame by comparison, though the energy crunch is reportedly thinning things out a bit.

The street signs were all in English. Many of the vehicles were U.S. Army surplus jeeps which Filipinos buy for very little and convert into mini-buses; they are called "jeepneys"—a cross between jeep and the British term for a mini-bus, which is "jitney"—and are about the cheapest form of public transportation. Each driver decorates his jeepney any way he wants, making several of them together on a street quite a colorful and often garish display.

Whenever our cab stopped—always with a screeching of brakes and gnashing of teeth in the frequently completely bottle-necked roadways—children would approach the car, peddling everything from homemade candy to newspapers to bootlegged American cigarettes. Jack bought a pack of what were allegedly Kents, but by the smell and taste, any resemblance was purely coincidental.

We passed by gigantic supermarkets, and one-man fruit stands; new skyscrapers, and ramshackle thatch houses; well-heeled businessmen and naked street urchins. The contrasts were apparent everywhere; I felt it deeply, and was awed by the dichotomy, the way I had been in London a few years before, while watching "Hair" at an historic Victorian theater.

The ride took about 25 minutes. The Tolentinos' home is located in a fairly well-to-do neighborhood by Filipino standards. The house is two stories, gray stucco, with a small garden, and the whole grounds surrounded by a high slatted fence. We knocked at the gate. An elderly, plump Filipino woman opened it cautiously and asked us to identify ourselves. We responded, and she smiled and unlocked the gate. We followed her across a concrete patio into the house. I thought at first she might be a servant, but no, it was Mrs. Tolentino. Her husband is a noted sculptor who until recently had been Director-General of the Philippine Christian Spiritualist Union, which is the full name of the Espiritista, the organization most of the Healers are associated with. The professor was ill and could not meet with us, but we were delighted to chat with his wife. There was something special about her—a certain inner glow, a quality we noticed in some of the Healers and their close associates that set them apart in a roomful of people.

We had seen the Hylands' movies of Tolentino's art studio, and were glad when Mrs. Tolentino invited us to see it. The studio is actually a converted garage. Statues and busts line the walls and tables, in various stages of progress. We could see what gave the professor his fine reputation—it's the way he captures people's eyes. You can almost sense that gray clay breathing, it is so lifelike: a Filipino boy who looked half angel, half demon, like small boys everywhere; stern-faced government officials; and a life-sized statue of Imelda Marcos, the Philippines' First Lady, wearing the traditional barong-tagalog gown with its characteristic stiff-winged, butterfly sleeves.

In this room, the Tolentino's Espiritista Center holds its weekly services. We'd heard reports of some strange goings on in the powerful vibrations of these spiritualists; for example, the Tolentinos have one of the world's largest collections of apports, which seem to be ordinary stones, but are said to have appeared from out of nowhere while mediums were giving readings. When hammered open, some of the apports were found to contain messages and Scripture written in Hebrew, a language virtually unknown in the Philippines.

We entered the main house through the back door and walked down a narrow hallway to a front room that was surprisingly cool and comfortable, probably because of heavy curtains that screened out the sun. The windows were adorned with wrought iron grill work, and overlooked the garden, where there was a tree with bright pink blossoms hanging limply in the heat. The manicured grass was withered. The few pieces of old furniture in the living room were well-worn, clean, and homey, and there were some throw rugs on the tile floor and a few pictures on the walls.

I asked Mrs. Tolentino if I could take a picture of her. She reluctantly assented, patting her gray hair into place. I focused the camera on her face, and suddenly the light meter in the camera went berserk—it would register at levels my photographer's instinct knew were incorrect, such as showing over-exposure in the dimly lit room; I took it out into the garden in the bright sunlight, and it came up underexposed. I was sick. I had been using the camera for two days without a hint of trouble (and for three years before that) plus, it had been thoroughly checked over before we left. There was nothing I could do, so I didn't get my photo of her. Mrs. Tolentino had an odd expression on her face, one I couldn't quite read.

As we talked, she was pleased and amazed that the four of us already had a pretty good idea of who the Healers were and how they worked. She was even more surprised that we, as Americans, knew about and agreed with their belief in reincarnation. We explained that we are a minority, just as the Philippine spiritualists are in the heavily Catholic country.

Mrs. Tolentino suggested that we talk to Leonora Pangan, the president of their Espiritista Center, for more data. She gave us an address and called a cab. On the way, I began fiddling with the camera, not really knowing what I was doing. Something was peculiar; as suddenly as it had gone on the blink, it was working again, once we left the Tolentinos' grounds. I should have expected it, since I had heard that strong psychic vibrations can play havoc with photographic and electronic equipment. It was the first time I had experienced it; it would not be the last.

Leonora Pangan works at the General Hizon Elementary School. We took the MacArthur Highway to get there, the first of many things we noticed in the Philippines named after the American general. (He's practically worshipped by the Filipinos for freeing them from the Japanese in World War II. President Truman isn't overly popular in the Philippines, therefore, despite the fact that he was in office when the Philippines gained independence from the United States.) We passed by an enormous monument with the golden figure of an angel perched on top. It was really striking, and we found out later it is one of the things Tolentino did on a government commission.

The school was large, imposing, four stories, looking much like a school building anyplace, but when we walked through the arched gate, we found ourselves in a sort of pseudo-Spanish central courtyard. We had no idea where to find Mrs. Pangan, so we stopped a woman in a white dress who happened to be walking by. It was Leonora. She had not been expecting us or waiting for us. It was one of those little quirks of timing that had to be precisely right—a little too pat to shrug off as coincidence; that's a convenient word, but it has little meaning! Leonora took our presence as a matter of course, as if four strange Americans walk in off the street and ask for her every day. (Had Mrs. Tolentino phoned her? We didn't think so.) But we could tell from the way some of the children were acting that it was rather unusual, because they giggled when they spotted us, and a group of them trailed after us into her office. The office really caught us off guard—Leonora, a spiritual healer, is the school nurse. In fact, she used to be a surgical nurse! She laughed when we asked if there was a conflict between her healing and her medical training. We knew that the attitude of most medical people toward the Healers is skeptical if not downright hostile. She pointed out that the two approaches can really complement each other when it comes to helping someone. She was right, of course, but we hadn't thought about it in that light.

Leonora, like Mrs. Tolentino, showed that Special Something, an intangible quality. She also exhibited another trait common among the Healers and their circle (actually among the Filipinos): a quiet kind of agelessness; she could have been anywhere from 30 to 60, though we guestimated late thirties. She was attractive, soft spoken, and warm. She chatted with us and gave us some material on Spiritualism to read while she worked. She was concerned that the kids were bothering us.

There were boys and girls ranging from about seven to twelve years old. They stood around us whispering and giggling among themselves in the universal manner of children. They all wore white shirts, the boys with dark blue long trousers and the girls with navy pleated skirts. For some reason, the oriental blood of the Filipinos seemed more apparent in the youngsters than in the adults, at least among the people we saw; their skin had a slightly more yellowish cast, compared to the varying shades of tan and brown of the grown-ups, and their eyes appeared to be a bit more slanted. They were unassuming and charming, chattering away in Tagalog, the Filipino polyglot language composed of smatterings of Arabic, English, Spanish, Polynesian, tribal dialects, Chinese, Japanese, Indonesian and whatever. They weren't bothering us. In fact, we were enjoying asking them questions about their school, which they answered shyly, at times with one of their number translating our English into Tagalog and vice versa. But we were obviously upsetting the routine. Leonora suggested we come back in about an hour when school ended for the day.

We decided to find some fresh fruit to eat, because we were hungry and thirsty and it had looked so tantalizing in the open-air markets we'd passed. But there was no sign of a restaurant or store; the area was undergoing urban renewal and was pretty well deserted. We didn't want to walk too far, because Jack's hip was bothering him. He was making an effort to ignore the pain and conceal the limp, but it was becoming more pronounced. Don and I tended to be solicitous towards him until we picked up the cue from Mary Ann that he really resented being babied.

People kept staring at us out of doors and windows, and toddlers and dogs seemingly materialized from out of nowhere and trailed along behind us. Where they all came from, we never did figure out! They were not begging or bugging us; it's just that we were a novelty in this neighborhood that few tourists go to. We trudged along for about three blocks, finally spotting a cab, which Don hailed. It stopped with a jerk—and the driver in the following car rear-ended it, so that ended that: the two cabbies started screaming at each other, and we were not about to be caught in the middle. There must be a traffic code in the Philippines, but apparently no one pays much attention to it, it's every man for himself—no blaming the snafus on women drivers, because you rarely see one!

We flagged another cab. The driver spoke no

English, one of the very few times we ran into a language barrier. But I told everyone not to worry, because I speak Spanish, which is the third language of the Philippines, behind Tagalog and English. So I asked him where we could get something cold to drink, having long ago decided we were more hot and thirsty than hungry. He couldn't answer; he didn't speak Spanish. (As a matter of fact, we didn't meet a single Spanish-speaking person on the whole trip. And come to find out, my Mexican Spanish would have been pretty much useless anyhow, Filipino Spanish being so riddled with eastern influences it is called "bamboo Spanish.") Our solution to the immediate problem was that good old standby, sign language. We went through the motions of eating and drinking. The driver's face lit up, and he laughed and nodded.

He pulled up in front of a grungy market place located in a large tent, that looked like something from a grade-B Hollywood backlot. But we figured it was time for an adventure. We paid him his few pesos (cabs are incredibly cheap in Manila), and in the four of us marched, hanging onto purses, tape recorder, cameras and each other for dear life. Most of the natives appeared to be in a state of shock at our mere presence. We were followed, again more out of curiosity than hostility. We were terribly uncomfortable, but there was this unspoken agreement among us: we must not lose face by walking out. We tried to act nonchalant as we strolled past the vending stands laden with fly-specked meat, cheap cotton clothes, rice cakes, and smelly fish. There was no market stall with anything vaguely resembling lunch in evidence. We tried hand signals again and the people steered, or rather pushed us toward a counter where a man was peddling a sickly-looking conglomeration of canned milk, sugar, and candied fruit in dirty plastic glasses. We speculated that we had nothing to lose but our appetites, so we tried it, seating ourselves at a counter near the booth. It was perfectly horrible. But we didn't dare leave it. Actually, if it hadn't been for that processed, white sugar, it might not have been too bad.

We asked for some water and were given glasses of ice water at once. In reaching for a water glass, Jack knocked over his punch. He looked relieved momentarily—until the man set a replacement down in front of him. We each drank about half of the stuff, and handed the vendor a five peso piece, about 75¢ American. We left without waiting for change. We were all a bit nervous, still thirsty and hungry, but laughing at our own misadventure. We had no trouble getting back to the school. Leonora asked us where we'd gone, then paled when we described the place. It was the Tondo market, which had a reputation as a notorious den of cutthroats. Before martial law, it was one of the most dangerous spots in the city, right in the middle of a ghetto of d.p.'s from the strife-torn southern islands. We might have gotten our heads knocked off if it wasn't for those extremely harsh new laws protecting tourists! We wouldn't have traded the experience, nor would we have wished it on our worst enemy. (It reminded me of the time I was one of a group of American students held under Russian machine guns at the Hungarian-Yugoslav border, incommunicado for 12 hours—at the same time the most terrifying and most fascinating part of that trip.)

Leonora asked us if we had time to come home with her, and of course, we jumped at the invitation.

Outside the school, we said goodbye to some of the little girls we had seen earlier. This time, they were holding stop signs and wearing badges and shoulder belts. Patrol girls, just like I had been in suburban Ohio at the same age!

Leonora flagged down a cab and we all piled in. She wanted to do some shopping on the way so we ended our typically harrowing ride in front of a fruit stand. Our mouths watered at the sight of that scrumptious, juicy fruit—mangos for about 15¢ apiece. Leonora debated then refused to buy them because they were too expensive! They would have been four times that at home, if you could find them at all, and after what we had just been through looking for cold fruit, we just stared at each other, mouths open. We didn't want to buy them ourselves for fear we would make her feel obligated or something, and besides, we were supposed to be waiting on the corner watching for a jeepney.

The jeepneys are a real experience. This one was red and yellow striped all around, with pink stenciled flowers here and there, and all kinds of streamers flying from the window posts. The inside was painted a gauche red-orange. Four benches ran the length of the vehicle from front to back, with barely enough room to get your legs in between. This was rush hour, so there were about 20 passengers at any given moment, scrapping for seats, crowding the aisles, and hanging on as best they could. The jeepneys have no set stops, although they do have fixed routes; you just get on wherever you like, and jump off anywhere along the route. It costs a few centavos, barely measurable in American money. People pass the fare and change back and forth to the driver and no one ever seems to cheat.

Our presence was apparently both an honor and a novelty to the natives. They squished over, and a few even got up so that we could all have seats. I was glad, because, being so tall, it would have been awkward to have to stand hunched over under the low canvas top of the jeepney. To the Filipinos, Americans are physical, spiritual and economic liberators. It is one of the few places left in the world you can go and be loved for being an American, not just cowtowed to for your dollars and secretly resented and despised. Memories of the cruel Japanese occupation during World War II are fresh; in addition, the U.S. controlled the Philippines with a beneficent iron thumb for the 40 years preceding World War II. So the Filipinos were excited about having a chance to talk to us young Americans, eagerly welcoming us to their country, and plying us with questions about ours. This went on for several blocks, until Leonora signalled us to jump off in a commercial district where we could catch a taxi out to the suburbs.

The Pangans' home is located in a middle-class housing project in Bulacan. The house is gray stucco, a rather small ranch style. It isn't fancy. It isn't even very well constructed. However, the Pangans are considered fairly well off by Filipino standards; both of them work, which accounts for their success, but it is unusual to find working wives and mothers out there.

THE INTERVIEW

When we went inside, Leonora asked if we would like something to drink. Would we ever! One of her daughters brought out a plate of homemade cookies and bottles of chilled mineral water. We sampled the pastries, but it was very hot out and it had been hours since we'd had a drink—we didn't even count that goop at the market—so we thought we would never get enough of that water!

Leonora was president of one Center of the Union Espiritualista Cristiana de Filipinas (Philippine Christian Spiritualist Union), better known as the Espiritista. She was also secretary of the national Espiritista, which is roughly equivalent to the Spiritualist Church in the U.S., with each Center like one congregation. But the Espiritista is chartered as a civic organization rather than a church, she explained, because of rather restrictive laws governing non-Catholic churches in the Philippines. There are several hundred Espiritista Centers in the country, most of which conduct healing services of some sort. Several dozen of them have psychic surgeons as their resident healing mediums.

Leonora was delighted to give us any information she could. Don and I had decided against lugging our tape recorder on the trip, but fortunately Mary

Ann and Jack had brought theirs. We asked Leonora if we could record her answers to a hastily scribbled list of questions we submitted to her. She agreed. Almost as soon as she began, the vibration in the room changed, becoming more or less charged. Her English improved at the same time. All of us seemed to be bordering on trance; I felt dizzy and at first thought it was heat and exhaustion, but later I knew better. Leonora spoke for nearly an hour, with us cutting in only to clarify our questions, or help her find the right word in English when she appeared to be groping. The following is a summary of what she told us:

The word "psychic" doesn't mean anything to Filipinos. They say "spirit gifts" (for example, "spirit surgery") to describe so-called psychic abilities. The people we westerners call "psychic surgeons" are known as simply "Healers" or "mediums." Sometimes they will say "faith healer" but without the same connotation we give it. Our term "faith healer" implies that the patient has to be a believer to be cured, whereas this is not necessarily the case with their kind of Spirit Healing.

There are three types of healing done in the Philippines. There is magnetic healing, in which the Healer transfers energy to the patient by massage or laying-on of hands. There is spiritual, in which the patient does not have to be present to receive help, because the regenerating energy is communicated by non-physical means, in other words, prayer or telepathic healing. Finally, there is material healing, which allegedly involves opening the body.

According to the Espiritista, there are some basic principles behind all healing: 1) God exists; 2) man is a creature of God and strives toward unity with

God by understanding natural laws and living in harmony with them; 3) the laws are unchanging, universal truths. Leonora went on to enumerate these laws: one is that an individual's identity continues after death, making it possible to communicate with the dead; another is that individuals are reborn time and again to help them learn what they need to know to become one with God—this is the Law of Karma; also, each individual has a responsibility to the physical and moral laws, the highest of which is the Golden Rule; lastly, the door to salvation, that is, to knowing God, is never closed to any soul.

All the things she was saying made sense to us and were very much what the American spiritualists believe (along with other reincarnationist religions such as some early Judaic and Christian sects, Hindus, Buddhists, etc.). She went on to clarify what she had already said, and give us an idea of what to expect from the Healers.

Spirit, she pointed out, manifests itself differently from culture to culture. In England, for example, messages are usually given to people by former friends or relatives who have passed away, through trance or voice mediums; in the Philippines, where nearly everyone has been raised Catholic, messages more often come from saints, archangels, or national heros. In any case, the medium utilizes a means that is least confusing and easiest for the people involved to identify with.

The Healers receive their abilities through Spirit Guides, beings that are sort of a link between God and mortals, what other churches may refer to as guardian angels. The Healers are very religious people who pray and sacrifice to get their power and ability, and if they abuse it, they will lose it. They can cure any person and any type of disease with one exception: they can not help a person whose illness has a purpose of teaching them something. They can not, in other words, interfere with that person's karma unless it is their own karma to do so.

By this time, the vibrations in Leonora's parlor were so heavy I had begun to shake. I was hot, then cold, which often happens to me in the midst of a psychic experience. Leonora sensed it. She put her hand on my forehead; the shaking stopped instantly, and my temperature went back to normal: she had done a quick, effective demonstration of magnetic healing, explaining that she was rebalancing my life forces. Then, after checking over our list of Healers' names, addresses and work schedules and making a few corrections, she said it was time for us to go. But first, she brought out a book for us to look at. It was the most beautiful, comprehensive anthology of spiritualist teaching we had ever seen, compiled and published by Joaquim Cunanan, the current Director-General of the Espiritista. We bought her copy then and there. She offered to get us a new copy the next day, but we decided we would rather have the one with her signature and vibrations. It was a large, hardcover edition but cost only 10 pesos, or about $1.50 American.

We walked down the stony, hilly roadway to the main highway, where we had no trouble getting a cab back to the hotel. As usual, the cab was a small Toyota, and we were quite cramped, but we didn't care, because it had been a most rewarding afternoon. It was about a half-hour ride across town during nerve-shattering evening rush—and cost under a dollar for the four of us!

It wasn't until we had cleaned up and gotten into

the dining room that we realized how famished we were. Don and I ate with his folks and the Mortons. The food at the Filipinas was fantastic and so was the service. We had a full course Chinese dinner from soup and appetizers to dessert and coffee; dinners were included in our tour package, but even if we had had to pay extra for it, it would only have been about $3.50 per person including tip. And this was a comparatively expensive place!

The Mortons and Don's parents had rested all day; now it was our turn. While they went to see what the Hilton Hotel looked like and do some souvenir hunting, we talked over the trip so far, and read excerpts from our new book, by-lined Edgar Cayce, Harry Edwards, et al. Then something occurred to us—we had been married almost three years, but this was the first time we'd ever taken a real trip, just the two of us. It was like a honeymoon, already bringing us even closer together.

VIRGILIO

We spent our second morning in the Philippines acting like typical tourists, sending postcards home, buying souvenirs, and generally wandering around wide-eyed. A friend of ours from Chicago had given us the phone number of Virgilio Gutierrez, a Healer she knew quite well; whoever answered the phone told us he would be working in nearby Quezon City, the capital of the Philippines, that afternoon. So the nine of us—Don's parents, the Mortons, Joe Bush, the Schmidts, and ourselves—piled into three cabs to go see him, and to actually witness psychic surgery for the first time. Virgilio's place wasn't hard to find, being a modern house in a suburban project. There were a number of cars parked in front, so we knew something must be going on. Other than that, it looked just like all the other homes on the block, a subdivision-type ranch-style. There was a 1958 black and white Buick in the driveway in almost mint condition; private cars are not driven as often or as hard in the Philippines, nor do they rust as much with comparatively little rain, and no snow and salt.

We went up the blacktop drive on foot. At the end was a large, plain room that originally had been the garage. About 50 people were seated on wooden benches, waiting, mostly quiet, some talking, some praying. At the far end of the garage was a much smaller room containing a plain, high table and an Espiritista banner on the wall behind it. There were several people in the little room, most of them women. But one man had to be Virgilio; the strong vibration drew our attention to him like a magnet. We were a good 40 feet away and couldn't make out what was happening. We slipped into some empty places on the benches, not knowing what to do, and stayed there about a half-hour, periodically standing or otherwise craning our necks to try to catch a glimpse of Virgilio at work.

Our presence was beginning to cause something of a stir among the waiting natives. That surprised us, considering the thousands of tourists from all over the world who visit the Healers each week. Of course, Virgilio was not the best known of the Healers, and also, not too many tourists actually go to the Healers' work places. Most of them just have the Healers come to the hotel, but we'd figured that wouldn't be sufficient to really get into what the Healers do, and get to know them personally.

There was a woman seated at a little desk near the doorway between the waiting room and the work room. She beckoned us forward and asked us to sign Virgilio's notebook, putting down our name, address, and what we wanted him to work on, then she led us through a side door and down a hallway to an enclosed porch just off the side of the workroom. Some other foreigners were already there, observing Virgilio through a louvered window; four were Germans, two Australians, and two were Japanese medical researchers. A Filipino man in a floral print shirt came in through a back door and introduced himself as Romeo Resureccion, president of this Espiritista

Center. Romeo briefed us about what we would be seeing. He said most foreigners are pretty nervous when they first visit the Healers, so he was trying to put us at ease and alleviate our fears. What fears? Don and I, at least, were only half aware of Romeo. We were too busy straining to look through the window into the room next door, where Virgilio, aided by his several female assistants, had been performing healing after healing, some magnetic, some body openings. The atmosphere was charged as we edged closer to get a good view.

We had seen films of psychic surgery a dozen times or more. We know people who have worked with various Healers, including Virgilio and thought that since we were well versed in the spiritual and physical principles of this healing phenomenon, not a thing would surprise us. We were wrong. Despite our preparation, witnessing psychic surgery in person for the first time was a mind blowing experience. Our mouths dropped open the first time we saw an opening done, much as we tried to take it in stride. I was afraid the real thing might be anti-climactic. But, no: we were to see hundreds of operations over the next two weeks. We tried to tune in on it, physically, mentally and spiritually, and although we came to accept it as natural, I don't think we ever took it for granted. That first day, as we tried to absorb it all in one sitting, we were stunned. It would be impossible to communicate that dizzying experience on paper, to fully describe the confusion, the vibrations, and the rush of people in and out as Virgilio worked. I don't even remember taking notes, but thank heavens I did, starting with my first impressions of Virgilio Gutierrez: mid-thirties, boyish, and very attractive, wearing an embroidered, sheer shirt of native barong-tagalog fabric and levis. An unruly shock of thick, wavy, blue-black hair kept falling over his forehead. But it was his eyes that showed how special he is: eyes like Don's—dark, deepset and penetrating, the disconcerting kind that can look right through you and sometimes make people uneasy.

Virgilio performs quickly and efficiently, in a classic style (if there is such a thing in psychic surgery). The first case we got a clear look at was an elderly Filipino woman, with an ugly, hard growth on her jaw about the size of a baseball. Romeo went to check in the notebook and came back with the information that the pain and swelling had kept the woman from eating for several days. She climbed up onto the table. The sheet had not been changed from the previous lord-knows-how-many patients, because the Healers just do not have to worry about the danger of infections; they don't need sanitary conditions when they work with Divine Power. As one of our acquaintances irreverently put it, "God is sterile!"

Virgilio asked the woman something in Tagalog. He is soft-spoken, and doesn't speak often—just enough to find out what he needs to know, and give some reassurance. He picked up a Bible from the foot of the table and read silently, lips moving, for a moment. Romeo told us he was using the Book of Daniel for his power that day. Next, Virgilio closed his eyes for a few seconds, apparently going into a brief, light trance. Eyes still closed, he prayed, and gently spread some coconut oil on the woman's jaw to lubricate the skin. He put his hand under her neck and lowered her onto the table face up. She said something to him and he opened his eyes and smiled slightly. His fingers probed the growth. The woman winced. He seemed to be massaging the skin, gingerly at first then a bit harder. There was a soft POP, a trickle of blood ran down her cheek, and Virgilio's left thumb and index finger were literally holding her skin open. He had used no instruments. The woman was relaxed but wide awake and evidently experiencing no discomfort. Using his right hand, Virgilio reached into the opening, which was approximately two inches long and a half inch wide, and pulled out a handful of squishy grayish tissue. He threw it into a pan of water held by one of his assistants, who was praying.

When Virgilio took his left hand away from the woman's cheek, the cheek closed up so fast we could barely see it happen. An assistant wiped away the traces of blood with a piece of cotton, leaving no scar or mark of any kind on the woman's face; the only sign that anything had been done was that the swelling was reducing right before our eyes, although her face was still puffy. Virgilio massaged it for about 30 seconds, rubbing some more of his oil in, then he helped the old lady sit up. She put her hand to her face to feel where the lump had been. She smiled broadly in gratitude and amazement. A relative dropped a few coins into the donation box in the waiting room before coming in and helping the woman out. Lapsed time for the whole procedure was less than two minutes. We didn't have time to muse on it. A woman's voice called out a name, and the next person on the list walked into the operating room. Virgilio rinsed his hands in a small dish and was ready to go again. (He often works with his hands wet, because water helps to conduct the healing energy.)

Few places in the Philippines aside from luxury

hotels have air-conditioning. It was extremely hot and close on that tiny porch, but we were better off than the folks in the main waiting room. At least we had an open roof, so there was some stirring of air; all they had was one electric fan that was hardly adequate to relieve even the people closest to it. I tried to ignore the heat and concentrate solely on Virgilio's work. As I began blocking everything else out, I felt myself drifting in and out of light trance. I was oblivious to everything for a while—I have no idea how long—until I felt something at my feet. I brought myself out and looked down to find a chicken pecking at my bare toes and sandal straps! I hadn't noticed before, but there were several birds on the porch, some scuttling around free and some in chicken wire cages. Virgilio's family must have been getting its own supply of fresh eggs, courtesy of a patient who couldn't afford to make a cash donation. I was sitting on a pile of wooden crates full of corn, so I moved away, over by a sink across the porch (perhaps 5 feet), figuring it was the feed the chicken was after. Well, that darned chicken followed me around like a puppy! I did not have the heart or inclination to shoo it away, but it soon tired of playing with the leather and left of its own accord.

The others had been talking with Romeo for quite a while; Virgilio was distracted by the conversation and signalled for silence. He walked out the side door of his operating room and onto the porch. I was watching him every step of the way, afraid that he was angry, but he just washed his hands in the sink next to me and casually lit up a cigarette. (Several of the Healers smoke, claiming they do not have to worry about diseases such as lung cancer!) Virgilio told us it would be our turn soon. I looked at my watch. Where the time had gone, I don't know, but we had been there a good two hours. Virgilio had performed dozens of operations in that time. I felt sorry for him; he was hot and sweaty and obviously tired. I had an urge to take out my handkerchief and wipe his forehead, but I didn't think that would be a very cool move. We chatted a while, passing on greetings from mutual friends and exchanging pleasantries. After about ten minutes, he was ready to return to work.

Most of the operations we had seen so far were similar to the one on the old woman, although hers was more dramatic than most because we could actually see the swelling shrink. For the next few minutes, we watched him remove some warts from a child's hand, cure a little girl's stomach ache with a magnetic healing, and take some blood clots out of a man's leg. The technique for the openings was always the same: rub some oil on the spot, massage, POP, hold it open with one hand while the other takes out whatever doesn't belong there, then remove both hands, leaving no marks, and rub on some more oil. And that's that—no muss, no fuss, no pain.

Most of the time, an assistant would read from the notebook to tell Virgilio what was wrong. Sometimes, he would do his own diagnosis, by putting a piece of paper or a white towel over the place where the person had the pain or problem. He would gaze through the towel as if it were an x-ray screen, and cock his head as if listening to a voice from far off—his Spirit Guide, I presume—instruct him on what was to be done. (The Healers all have their own diagnostic tricks, like reading auras, or being clairvoyant or clairaudient, etc.)

It wasn't easy to see what was going on from

where we were standing, so Romeo was still trying to fill us in. He finally steered us away from the observation window and began what amounted to a sermonette on healing, which paralleled what we already knew and what we had learned from Leonora. Don decided to skip it and try to get some movies; I stayed and took notes, while he went into the operating room. He came back a short time later. It had been a hopeless task because every time he would get a good angle, somebody would get in the way of the lens or would cast a shadow and make it too dark to get good pictures. He put the photo gear back in the case.

Romeo's lecture included the following: he referred to Virgilio as "the medium" because God's power is channeled through the Healers. According to Romeo, there are three other forms of mediumship: first, there is the medium who knows what is happening in other times and places through astral travel; second, there's the medium who receives messages through automatic writing; and thirdly, the voice medium, who imparts messages from the dead. "Mediums," he went on, "are initiates of God. They are on earth—this time—for the purpose of studying the higher reality of God's relationship to Man and Man's relationship to God." A highly simplified explanation, but beautiful and valid.

The woman with the notebook was calling out a name, over and over. It finally dawned on us that it was a heavily accented "Don Sladek;" Virgilio was now taking the foreigners and Don was to be the first. Most of the foreigners aside from the nine of us had left long ago, having come to watch and apparently not wanting any subjective experience to go along with their scientific observations.

Don wanted his hearing improved and had written that in the book; his left ear had suffered nerve damage 20 years earlier from having been on the army rifle range while he had measles, and though his hearing had been tested periodically over the years, there was nothing the doctors could do to help it. Virgilio must have needed to know more than the medical diagnosis. He told Don to lay on his back on the table. Virgilio pushed Don's head to the side, and looked at the area behind the ear through a sheet of paper. He said there were blood clots in the neck that were blocking circulation to the ears, and that he would get rid of them, which would put the healing process in motion. It made sense, for Don had had trouble with his neck, too, for years, with it being all tense and knotted up.

I stood directly across from Virgilio on the other side of the table, taking pictures as he worked, first with the still camera, then movies. He directed Don to turn over on his side so he could work on the flat surface behind the ear. He stuck his fingers just behind and a little under the ear and wriggled them for a few seconds; a single drop of blood splashed softly on the sheet. Virgilio withdrew his hand. He held it out for us to see—several tiny, dark, crusty "cysts," as he termed them, lay on his fingertips. He tapped Don on the shoulder, and Don, declaring that he had not felt anything at all, sat up and rubbed the spot. Where previously there had been a small, hard, sore lump on his neck, there was nothing at all: it was the first time we knew for certain that something had actually been removed in psychic surgery; this operation, at least, could not possibly have been a fake. Don took off his wristwatch and put it up to his ear, but he still could not hear it tick. Improvement isn't always instantaneous, we knew, especially for something as long-standing as that hearing problem, but he was hoping anyway.

It was my turn. I had written in the book that I wanted something done to stop severe menstrual cramps, and also to correct my extreme nearsightedness (about 20/200 in the left eye and 20/150 in the right, corrected with contact lenses to about 20/30 and 20/40). Virgilio asked me to lie on my back on the table so he could do a magnetic healing on my eyes (no opening). Like Don, I didn't expect miracles or a one operation cure for my 20-year old problem, but at least this was a start.

I looked up at Virgilio and noticed his eyes roll back and close. He hadn't done or said a thing, but something odd was beginning to happen—I felt myself drifting off. While he massaged my forehead and eyes with coconut oil, I found myself floating among strange people at scenes and places I couldn't identify. It was very comfortable, and I didn't really want to get up when Virgilio tapped me on the shoulder and said, "Okay." I sat up, stared at him, and blurted, "I've known you before." He not only did not reply, but gave no indication he had heard me at all. I was afraid he thought it was a come-on or something, so I dropped it, asking instead if he saw anything else wrong with me. He asked me to come back later in the evening when it was less crowded, as he wanted to remove "cysts" from my spleen, ovaries, appendix and breast; he determined these things entirely on an intuitive, psychic level, without examining me.

Marge Morton was next. She was awfully nervous to begin with, plus being skeptical and confused at what we'd been watching all afternoon, which was understandable. Romeo commented that it was a shame she couldn't relax more, as she would get a lot more help if she were less uptight. (Yes, he used the word "uptight.") It's not that you have to be a believer in order for the Healers to help you; it's just that tension tends to create negative vibrations that may diffuse their power or distract them to an extent. Marge was on her back on the narrow table, staring up wide-eyed at the ceiling, her hands in the air at a right angle to her body, arms bent stiffly at the elbows; the table was too narrow for her to put them comfortably at her sides, as she is larger than most of the Filipinos who use the table. (I had a similar problem, being six feet tall. My legs hung over the end of most of the Healers' tables!)

Marge had not told Virgilio anything specific she wanted done. But he picked up psychically that something was causing a problem in her abdomen. He took a couple of deep breaths and went into trance for a brief time, again seeming to listen to something. When he came out of it, he said that blood and clots left in her womb from before menopause were pressing into various organs, causing swelling, and aggravating her colitis. It was quite different from a medical explanation of colitis—which Marge confirmed had been diagnosed by doctors—but the Healers are not medical people and often put things in terms far removed from what the doctors say. Sometimes they'll give a plausible reason for an ailment whose cause is unknown to medical science or which, like colitis, could have different causes; more often, they'll use words such as "blockage," "belly-knot" and "grease-bag" because unless they've been around westerners a great deal, they will not know "colitis," "ulcer" or "cyst." Formal education and formal semantics or not, they do get at least some degree of results in a majority of patients!

Virgilio suggested that Don set up the camera again, to try once more to get decent films without having heads in the way and shadows messing up the lighting. Virgilio went to work—and it was one of the most spectacular operations we saw on the trip. He moved very quickly, his hands lightly running over Marge's stomach in double-time. He rubbed coconut oil around her abdomen, making circular motions in tightening patterns with his left hand. Suddenly his right hand shot downward and we heard that little popping sound. Rivulets of blood ran down Marge's side, more bleeding than we had seen in any psychic surgery thus far, yet still remarkably little. His right hand went deeper into her body, while the left held back the edges of the opening. Standing right next to the table, we could see clearly the layers of muscle tissue inside. There were soft squishing sounds as Virgilio flipped part of what appeared to be the intestine out of the opening, holding it down on the outer surface of her belly between his fingers. He began removing goop with his other hand. We could see well into the abdominal cavity, but there was hardly any bleeding after that initial spurt. There was no way Virgilio could have been faking this, no way it could have been sleight-of-hand.

Don was taking pictures with the Super-8 low-light camera, using high-speed film without any auxiliary lighting. Virgilio asked him to move next to him on the opposite side of the table for a better angle, but apparently Don was so wrapped up that he didn't hear him, so Romeo took Don's arm and tried to steer him, then pull him. Don would not budge, even when I shoved his shoulder, it was as if he were riveted to that spot. We finally gave up, knowing that despite the fact he was shooting film like crazy, he was in deep trance!

Virgilio asked an assistant for a pan of water. With his right hand, he reached deep into Mrs. Morton's abdomen pulling out several stringy, reddish clumps of bloody material; they were not quite clots, neither were they liquid. He kept scooping this kind of stuff out into the pan with his right hand, while his left kept her skin open. He called for cotton, and stuffed a huge wad into the hole, then brought part of it back out, soaked in blood. Mrs. Morton was wide awake and making occasional comments, but she was still very nervous and refused to look down to see what was going on.

Virgilio said he was going to leave the rest of the cotton inside her to soak up impurities. He quickly took away both hands, and the wound closed up right in front of us. One of the women who works with Virgilio took a rag and cleaned off Marge's abdomen. There was no sign of anything remaining. Virgilio had gone to wash his hands. When he came back, he smoothed some coconut oil on the spot where he had operated, and did a brief magnetic healing, explaining that the magnetic energy helps the body to start regenerating itself after an operation or any kind of imbalance of life forces. He instructed Marge not to drink coffee for a few days, and not to lift anything heavy. She got up and walked away. Total time was under four minutes.

It was stifling hot and I had to get to a washroom. I asked where it was and one of the women led me into the main part of the house. The john didn't flush and there was no toilet paper, yet this was a fairly nice neighborhood; in the Philippines, indoor plumbing as we know it is a luxury reserved for the rich, even in the big cities, because of expense and low water pressure.

Virgilio's father was sitting at the kitchen table. I wanted some fresh air so he directed me to the door, past the living room. After a few minutes outside, I turned to go back in, and spotted Virgilio's father leaning out of the paneless picture window that faced the driveway where I was standing. Behind him, on the wall opposite the window, hung an enormous blowup of a black and white photo of Virgilio. It was excellent, perfectly capturing those magnificent eyes. I asked his father who had taken it, and he told me a psychic researcher from California. There was a spark of pride in the older man's voice when he spoke about his son, so I pumped him for further information.

Virgilio was raised in a Spiritualist household, and his father takes credit for raising him in an environment that encouraged him to become a Healer. The house is Virgilio's family home, but he doesn't live there anymore because of all the people whom he either could or would not turn away coming to him day and night for help; he has to rent a room elsewhere in order to get his much-needed rest. He works in Quezon City on Sunday, Monday and Tuesday, and also works in Pansanjan Province, saving his donation money for a healing center for the natives there. (He never asks for money. You just leave it anonymously in the box in the waiting room, anything from a couple of pesos for impoverished Filipinos to five, ten, even twenty dollars from American tourists. Generosity of the foreigners is the only way he'll ever get that new chapel.)

Pretty soon, the rest of our group wandered out. Virgilio was all through for the afternoon, having worked on Jack, Dad, Joe and Nate while I was out-side; he wanted to see Dad, Jack, Mary Ann, Nate and me again. We stood around talking for a few minutes while Virgilio posed for snapshots. We'd asked the cab drivers to come back for us at five and they showed up promptly. We were all very quiet and thoughtful on the return ride.

Back at the hotel, Don and I sorted it all out. Don asked what had impressed me the most that after-noon, which was easy—it was watching Nate while Virgilio did that fantastic operation on his wife. I had seen him undergo a true transformation: his ex-pression changed, his features softening as he wit-nessed a miracle happening to a loved one; tears welled up in his eyes, and his attitude towards the rest of us altered perceptibly; he became less aloof, more open, less aware of his material wealth. I had even noticed a change in his aura as his whole vibra-tion became more sympathetic and tolerant. I was deeply moved. Imagine my surprise when ordinarily sensitive Don declared he hadn't noticed!

For him, Don said, the most impressive event was the stomach operation on the Filipino woman. He expressed hope the films would turn out well. I said, "That must have been while I was outside, I didn't see such an operation." Don replied, "Of course you did. Virgilio worked on her right after you." I honestly did not know what he was talking about. "You know," he said, "the one where I was taking films standing on a chair." Somebody was confused. Virgilio had worked on all of us together, with no natives in between. And there was no chair in the room, only a wobbly bench that he had tried to shoot from for a couple minutes and given up because it was too shaky and far from the table. So I said,

"Well, I don't know about that one, but wasn't it something the way he worked on Mrs. Morton?"

Now it was my turn to be confused, because Don claimed he had not seen that one. But he couldn't have missed it—he was right beside me the whole time, standing there taking pictures! It dawned on us simultaneously: we were talking about the same operation, but Don, in trance, had seen the patient as a small oriental woman in a floral print dress, while I had seen only Mrs. Morton, an American in white shorts and pink blouse. I knew Don was going through something significant during that operation, because of his refusal to budge when Romeo and I had tried to move him around, but little did I realize he was having an astral projection! He had seen the whole thing from the ceiling (which is why he thought he was standing on a chair) while physically shooting from the floor, and had apparently seen her in a past life.

It was too much. We burst into hysterical laughter, partially because we were tired, and partially from the sheer joy of realizing what a psychically unique, uplifting experience this trip already was, on only the second day. We were still in hysterics when we went down to dinner. We didn't explain to the others, not that we could have even if we'd tried, they would have thought we were nuts, for sure! (Incidentally, the film sequence of that particular operation is one of the best we got!)

VIRGILIO II

Dinner was a fiasco, mainly because the travel agency rep showed up at the hotel dining room and threw a monkey wrench in the works. Our travel agent in Chicago had made our arrangements through an agency in San Francisco, which in turn was using Diplomat Travel in Manila. The girl from Diplomat informed us there would be a change in plans: instead of staying in Manila for a full week, we would be leaving for Baguio in two days; that meant we would not be able to look up a number of other Healers we wanted to see in the Manila area, nor could we make follow-up visits. Don argued that we wanted to stick to our original plans of a week in Manila and a week in Baguio and the lowlands, but he couldn't get through to her, as her English was terrible and she wasn't too bright or experienced to begin with. Don was getting angry. He was semi-official spokesman for all of us, on account of his refusal to let anybody push him around. He was nice about it, but firm; this tour was supposed to have been unstructured except for a couple of set appointments with Tony, Marcello and Mercado the next week. And now the travel agency was playing games with us.

We didn't have time to reason with them then,

since we were due back at Virgilio's. He wanted to work some more on several of us—but what he had told Mary Ann was particularly intriguing. There was nothing wrong with her, Virgilio had said, he just wished to help her develope her own "spirit gift."

We decided to hire a couple of private cars and drivers for the evening, having heard how hard it can be getting cabs at night in the Manila area. Don found the young Filipino who had approached us at the entrance to the hotel when we'd first arrived. Again, it was no coincidence that this man was the one we hired to take us around, or rather, who had first asked us for the job. He turned out to be much more than a chauffeur—he was guide, translator and above all, friend. His name is Rotillo Kho—Boykho to us—and we liked him immediately. He's a character, bubbly, talkative, full of historical trivia and tidbits of local gossip, a hustler in the most positive sense of the word. (Altogether quite true to his Aries sun sign.) He's small but wiry, boyish looking, with tousled hair almost to his shoulders. We judged him to be in his early twenties, but that Filipino agelessness fooled us. He was 33.

The Schmidts piled into Boykho's little green Toyota with us. Boykho had arranged for another car and driver for the rest of the group, so they followed us. There were only a few people at Virgilio's when we got there. Romeo greeted us warmly and asked us to wait for a few minutes while Virgilio finished with them. While we were waiting, his main assistant, Sister Rose, came out and nicely asked us if we would be interested in please buying some raffle tickets from her for a benefit for the International Red Cross. Why not? It was for a good cause and a whole book was only $1.50 American, so we each bought a book. Mrs. Morton seemed to be angry about it for some reason, as if that little bit of money for charity was an imposition. We ended up filling out the stubs in various Healers' names and giving them the drawing slips over the next few days. We never heard if any of them won the grand prize of a color television, or even if they understood what the tickets were!

A few minutes later, Virgilio called us into the operating room. He ordered Mary Ann to sit in the chair across the table from him. When she was comfortable, he reached over the table and touched her forehead and told her to pray. It was silent for a moment, as both of them closed their eyes and meditated, then Virgilio advised her to work with a crystal ball to develop her psychic potential, mentioning that he uses a crystal ball as the focal point for his own meditation. He took her into the main part of the house and showed it to her; she reported he keeps it under water in a fish tank to protect it from bad vibrations. I was trying to take pictures of Virgilio working with Mary Ann—I say trying, because my Nikkormat was doing what it had done at the Tolentinos': when I aimed it at him, the light meter went crazy. Fortunately I was able to judge the settings pretty well anyway, and the photos came out all right.

Sister Rose Lukban Penson, who had sold us the raffle tickets and is a sensitive herself, told Mrs. Morton that at least two people in our group have "the gift," to be able to heal others. According to Marge, Rose mentioned no names; nevertheless, it was an exciting thing to hear, more so since Don and I had been experimenting with healing for several months, curing each other's headaches and things

like that as we'd been taught by our friend Deon
Frey, a well known medium.

Rose is a story herself. She is about 40 years old,
a registered pharmacist, and exudes a kind of quiet
energy that has a calming effect. Several years ago,
she went to watch Virgilio work, out of curiosity. She
had no spiritualist background, but Virgilio informed
her that she had been his "spirit mother" in a past
life in Tibet and asked her to stay and help him. She
refused, but she was drawn back; the next time he
asked her to stay, she did. Much to the chagrin of her
family and professional associates, she gave up her
pharmaceutical practice and became a Healer.

By now, everyone in our group seemed to be
opening up to what was happening, unconsciously
tuning in on the good vibrations, though with some,
the change was barely perceptible and didn't last,
and with others, it was more dramatic. Don's mother
was getting along very well with Romeo. He even
promised to have his wife make us some blessed coconut oil like Virgilio uses. It is supposed to be good to
use whenever you have any kind of pain; you just rub
it on the way the Healers do. Romeo was planning to
visit Chicago the next fall so we told him to look us
up, and we'd get him some speaking engagements.
But he never came; he must have had trouble getting
an exit visa.

He asked if we had any friends or relatives back
home whom Virgilio might help by what he called,
"absent healing," a form of prayer in which the
Healers project positive vibrations or psychic energy
to others during nightly meditation, at times even
visiting patients on the astral plane. They use it to
work on those who can't come to them, to prepare
people whom they will be seeing in the future, and to

follow up on cases. We left several names and addresses. Romeo said it would have been even better to give Virgilio their pictures, but we hadn't brought any with us. He showed us a photo of a man whom the Schmidts identified as a minister friend of theirs who had been to the Philippines and was showing his films back in Minnesota.

Virgilio and his assistants—whom we facetiously referred to as his "groupies"—had done a magnetic healing on Dad's chest that afternoon, and Sister Rose had massaged it for about twenty minutes. Virgilio gave him another treatment in the evening, going into a light trance and praying while running his hands over the entire chest in distinct patterns. (Chakra to chakra in figure eights and circles—that is, causing energy to flow from one psychic center of the body to another and back.) Rose, the only one of Virgilio's female assistants who was still there, massaged Dad's chest again for a few minutes. He seemed to be feeling much better. He was a little breathless, but the pains were gone and he was laughing and joking about Rose being his "new girl friend."

Nate was next. He climbed up on the table Dad had vacated so that Virgilio could take care of his hernia. That would be a great relief to Nate, who has to do a lot of heavy lifting in his scrap iron business. He loosened the waist of his slacks and pulled his shirt up around his ribs, the same limited undressing that Dad had done for his chest work and Marge had done earlier for her abdominal surgery. Virgilio looked at Nate's lower abdomen through a sheet of paper. The operation itself was very brief, perhaps a minute and a half. With rapidly moving hands, Virgilio opened up the area, put one hand into the body in a sort of twisting motion, and brought out a clump of something. He kept the other hand inside for a few seconds and it looked like he was twisting or stretching something. He pulled out his hand and the opening disappeared. Nate reported marked improvement in his condition after that, and the hernia has not troubled him since.

My turn again. This time, I asked if everybody would mind leaving. Up to now, we had all watched each other's operations and dozens of other people had seen us worked on in the afternoon, but Virgilio had said he was going to take something out of my breast. I made a joking remark about not wanting our films to be x-rated, afraid their feelings might be hurt, but they all understood. This was the first time any of us or anyone we'd seen had to really undress for an operation. Usually, you just uncover your midsection or leg or whatever and there is no need for modesty. I unfastened my jeans, because Virgilio was going to check my ovaries, and propped myself up on my elbows so I could watch. He put a little oil on my stomach. Then he prayed. With very little machination, he reached into the left side of my body over the ovary, and brought out a blood clot; he did the same thing on the right side. There was almost no bleeding, and all I felt was a slight pinching. I carried on a conversation with him and Don for the couple of minutes the whole thing took. Then I lay flat on my back, unbuttoned my blouse, and unhooked my bra, but took nothing off. Sister Rose supported my left shoulder so I could turn to the side a little and watch what Virgilio was doing. I didn't even feel him making the opening on the side of my breast. The only thing I felt was a tickling as a trickle of blood ran into my armpit. Virgilio stuck just the little finger of his right hand into the tiny hole he had made; when he withdrew it, there was a white, irregular piece of tissue on the tip. And it was all over.

The vibrations were very powerful by now. Virgilio said he wanted to work some more on my eyes. I closed them and was in trance almost immediately. I started seeing the same scenes and people I'd seen that afternoon in even more detail, but I still wasn't able to make anything of it. I also saw sporadic flashes of light at various spots in both eyes. When I saw the films, that was easy to figure out: Virgilio had given me what the Healers call "spiritual injections," by first making hand motions as if holding a hypodermic needle, then using the Bible to fill it the way a doctor uses a vial of serum. He pushed the "imaginary" plunger of the hypo. But the energy transfer is not imaginary; you can really feel it, very concentrated, wherever they give you the "shot." The places he put that spirit needle tip were precisely the points where I'd seen the flashes of light inside my head, and felt a warm tingling. Virgilio had not hypnotized me or anything, and most people do not go into trance or have an extraordinary experience while the Healers work on them. Of course, I was already used to trance because of Don's and my prenatal regression sessions; while Virgilio worked on me, I was way under and very reluctant to come out of it when he was done. He sensed that something was happening to me and probably knew what it was; he looked at me very intently for a few seconds then opened his mouth as if to say something. Apparently, he changed his mind, for he walked away without uttering a word.

Don and I rejoined the others in the waiting

room. There was a man in an army uniform there, whom Virgilio introduced as Colonel somebody-or-other. He was a government official, and questioned us closely about where we came from and why we were at Virgilio's. He was nice about it in a gruff, military sort of way, but he seemed rather protective towards Virgilio, like he wanted to make sure we weren't going to cause him any trouble. We knew that the Healers are talked about openly in the Philippine press and that their work is not only encouraged but licensed by the federal government. They've even operated at the Presidential Palace if news reports and rumors are true.

It was about 9:00 p.m. The colonel reminded us that there was a midnight curfew under martial law lasting until 4 a.m. We still had plenty of time to get back to the hotel, so we stayed and talked a few moments longer. This was Tuesday night; we promised Virgilio we would try to make it back for his weekly Espiritista service on Sunday if we were still in town.

BLANCE

We were really curious about Juan Blance because of the conflicting things we'd heard about him—that he was one of the great Healers, and that he was a drunk who often couldn't help people at all. He works early every morning, so we arranged for Boykho to pick us up after breakfast. Jack and Mary Ann went with us, while Nate, the only other member of our group with enough spirit of adventure to get moving so early, followed in a cab. We drove for about a half hour, out of the city and province of Manila, into Rizal province. On this ride, the paradoxes of the Philippines were more apparent than ever, with modern buildings next to historic Spanish ones; new cars tailing horse carts; and huge, modern hospitals just minutes from Healers' homes. (Only the rich can afford the hospitals. That's one reason the Philippine government appreciates what the Healers do—providing cheap health care for peasants who have no˜ access to the very limited social services.) But perhaps the most obvious contrast was in a congested market place, where a rickety horse cart was tied to a post in front of a store bearing the sign—in English—"Suburban Hardware." It was the kind of place you'd expect to see a late model station wagon.

Blance's house is a good-sized, two story, white stucco and frame place. The family lives on the second floor of the building. The workroom and anteroom take up half the lower level; occupying the other half is a sort of sundries counter where his children sell gum, candy, school supplies, etc. to supplement the scanty income he receives from healing. A daughter was working at the stand that morning.

A teenaged boy came out of the house. He looked exactly like the pictures we had seen of Blance, minus 20 years and about 50 pounds, obviously his son. He asked us what we were there for—as if he didn't know—and told us the Healer would be down in a few minutes. He led us into the waiting room, which we entered by going down a couple of steps and through a doorway so low I had to duck to avoid hitting my head. Blance works every day, so his average patient load is smaller than Virgilio's, and he doesn't need as much space. The waiting room was about 12 feet by 18 feet, with concrete floor painted red, and a half dozen low, slatted chairs with carvings on the arms and backs which had been donated by a satisfied patient. The only other furniture was a rough coffee table, and a dusty dresser with a cracked mirror. A doorway on the far wall led to the operating room. There was one thing that was startling, however—posters from Walt Disney feature cartoons on the walls: two Cinderellas, a Snow White, and some promotional photos from various other Disney films. They were so incongruous in that setting, but they did add some color and distinction to the place. We never thought to ask where they came from because it just did not seem important.

By now it was a little after 7 a.m. and we were all pretty sleepy yet. I got up to use the bathroom, having to go through the operating room to get to it. The operating room was small—barely enough room for three people to move around, with the table standing under a tiny, high window and an Espiritista banner similar but not identical to the one at Virgilio's hanging at the head of the table. On the opposite wall was a calendar with the picture of a bull fighter. Like the posters in the waiting room, it seemed out of place. The toilet consisted of a hollowed out mound of dirt covered by a wire screen. As I was coming out, I literally bumped into a grinning Juan Blance, who had just come into the operating room from the waiting room, bringing the others in tow. I liked him immediately. He's a roly-poly, jovial man with a pot belly that some say comes from beer drinking. (He reminded us of our good friend Jack Gorham, Don's naprapath.) It was a different kind of vibration from Virgilio's, but equally positive and strong in its own way.

There was a little small talk while we told Blance hello from the Hylands, and got his permission to take movies. Then he pointed at Nate and directed him to get up on the table; his English was very broken, so he used a lot of hand signals. Nate lay face down with his head on the musty, lumpy pillow. Blance ordered him, "Pull up shirt. I take cyst from back." Don nodded that he had the camera ready, and before I realized what was happening, Blance grabbed my left hand, extended the forefinger, and pointed it at Nate's back; I felt a warm tingling in my arm all the way to the elbow. We were standing several feet away from Nate, and I hadn't even touched him. Juan said, "Look." Astonished, we watched a thin, red line appear on the lower right side of Nate's back, starting as a speck and moving slowly upward until the cut was about an inch long. Blance was laughing at our reaction to what we were seeing. John Hyland had told us that Blance gets a kick out of using other people's hands to make his openings, but feeling that transfer of power, and seeing the results of that healing energy as it runs through you is something of a shock, as well as a thrill.

The actual operation was a combination of psychic surgery and folk medicine. First, a folk method: Blance took a gold coin (Spanish, circa 1898, which he uses for sentimental reasons) and placed it directly on the cut. He then soaked a piece of cotton in alcohol and put it on the coin. He struck a match and lit the cotton, and quickly inverted a shot glass over the whole thing, creating a vacuum in the glass to force foreign material toward the surface. (We understand this technique—known as "cupping"—is a home-style remedy for snakebites, carbuncles and all sorts of things in many places in the world.) Nate's skin swelled up into the glass, pushing the coin up at a slant, but there was almost no bleeding through the opening; the psychic surgery aspect was taking over as Blance took away the glass, cotton, and coin. He rubbed three fingers of his right hand over the tiny slit in Nate's back, now a bit swollen. We asked Nate if he felt anything, and he described a slight sting when the skin opened but that was all. Blance, meantime, was doing a play-by-play of the operation for Nate. The next step was to gently probe the opening with thumb and forefinger. A slimy grayish strip of something slid up out of the cut, through the Healer's fingers, and onto Nate's back almost by itself. Blance said it was waste material that had been blocking circulation to the back and formed the little lump Nate had been concerned about. We asked if it were a cyst. Blance shrugged his shoulders. He told us it might not have looked like that, in one piece, in the body; he just brought it all together in a clump because it was easier that way. It was about ½" wide and ¾" long, and sort of waxy. He passed it around for all of us to look at before tossing it in the trash can under the table. None of us thought to ask if we could take it to be analyzed.

Blance's openings do not close the way most of the Healers' do. When he wiped away the slight amount of blood from around the cut, the opening did not disappear. He put a piece of damp cotton on it and told Nate to get up. He said the mark would eventually go away, but he likes to leave a reminder of his work. That was true, as all of us whom he worked on were to find out; the split in the skin usually heals in a few days, just like a regular cut, then it turns into a thin, red line which normally becomes an almost invisible, slightly jagged white scar. He's the only Healer we saw who works like that, leaving any evidence of the extraordinary phenomenon.

After working on Nate, Blance allowed us to observe as he took a lump off the neck of a Filipino teenager, and took some blood clots from along a crippled old man's spine. For each patient, he followed the same procedure step by step, using the coin-cotton-shot glass, then removing the whatever.

Naturally, we were curious about the chances of infection when he works on somebody without sanitary conditions, then sends them away with an open wound like that. But he said none of his openings ever gets infected, nor is there ever death or complications. It was the same explanation we got at Virgilio's: though the Healers do not take sanitary precautions, there is no danger, because the energy that is channeled through them is from the purest source there is—God. If there were any hint of a problem, the power simply would not come through and they would be unable to work on that particular case. That's why they can use the same sheets, pans, etc. for patient after patient. They do make an effort to keep their workrooms clean and neat, but it is not necessary to sterilize. They do use a lot of water and alcohol and/or some kind of natural oil, but that is for lubricating the skin and conducting the energy rather than for cleanliness.

Blance was really personable and he seemed to enjoy chatting with us; there was amusement in his voice, but not derision or condescension. He's just a happy kind of person who doesn't take either himself or his work overly seriously.

Nate, Mary Ann and I are all nearsighted, and therefore had to have our eyes cleaned out, which Blance said would allow the healing processes to work better to correct the vision. Chicago pollution had been playing havoc with my eyes. They would not water; whenever I got something in my eye it would get caught under my contact lens and scratch the cornea. I'd been wearing contacts fairly comfortably for 10 years, but Blance said they were partly to blame, explaining that they were pressing in on my eyeballs, which in turn was choking the tear ducts. I wasn't wearing my lenses on the trip, because I figured I'd have to be taking them out a lot for healings. Blance removed my glasses and handed them to me. I sat in a chair as he propped my right eye open with his left thumb and forefinger. I felt nothing at first, then my eye felt much like it did when I took out a contact—that is, I felt it relax, and there was a simultaneous lessening of pressure inside my head. I felt the tension easing, starting deep in the center of my head, and sort of pushing forward till it reached the eye. I heard the others gasp (I did, too, when I saw the films) as a marble sized ball of gunk rolled out of the inner corner of my eye. Blance plucked it up with his right hand and showed it to me, describing it as mucus that had gathered around particles of pollution trapped in back of my eye. He said it had been scattered throughout the channels of the eye, but he had made use of a natural opening (the corner of my eye) to bring it together and out. The instant it hit the surface, my eye began to water for the first time in six months. (An eye doctor later informed me that there is a medical procedure to remove this type of clutter from in and around the eyes, so there may be a scientific basis for what Blance did in this particular case.)

I watched as Blance did the same thing on Mary Ann and Nate. He never actually touched their eyes, except for holding open the lid so the stuff could roll out freely. We all agreed—it was beautiful and incredible, and also impossible to fake. We had all actually felt the material traveling forward in our heads, then experienced a relief of pressure as it slipped into the little space between the eye and the top of the nose.

Don was next in line. He was always getting headaches and stiff necks, and had various pains in his back and neck, and even a full year of weekly naprapathic treatments had not broken up the calcium deposits that were the apparent cause of it all. He lay face up on the table. Blance pressed the fingers of one hand into one side of the front of Don's neck, and poked and twisted with his forefinger, his hand wide open the whole time. A big chunk of waxy stuff which Blance identified as mucus popped out right through the skin. There was no actual opening at all! Blance repeated the same motions on the other side of the throat, this time showing Don the stuff that came out before throwing it away. Don couldn't believe it, having felt nothing aside from the pressure of Blance's hand on his throat.

Blance turned to me again, for I had mentioned a tendency to headaches, too. He indicated that part of my eye trouble was due to poor circulation to the head and that he was going to clear out some of the "garbage" contributing to it. I was face down on the table, but I knew exactly when he made the opening, because I felt the cut forming on the back of my neck below my right ear. It stung a little, much like a paper or razor cut. I didn't see whose hand Blance used to make the opening; he had been alternating among Jack, Don, Mary Ann and me all morning. He did his bit with the shot glass, etc. on my neck. I felt him digging around the hole. It was not painful; I was simply aware that something was there. He pulled out a piece of something that looked a lot like what he'd removed from Don's neck. By now it was apparent that a lot of people probably have a lot of material in them that doesn't belong, probably accumulations from poor diet, too little exercise, pollution, and what all. It's particularly prevalent, according to Juan Blance, among people who live in big cities, and although not really dangerous in itself, it possibly adds up to the point where it either indirectly causes or aggravates a good many other physical disorders.

You do not have to have anything seriously wrong in order to get help from the Healers. You hear a great deal about people who go to the Philippines and are cured of cancer, heart disease and so on, but the Healers can also get rid of those annoying little things that would be infeasible or expensive for a doctor to bother with. For example, Blanche turned chiropractor to alleviate one of Don's ailments. Doctors had told Don his left leg is ⅜ of an inch shorter than the right. Most people have some difference but it usually doesn't cause any problem; Don does a lot of walking and one foot was giving him almost constant trouble, most likely from standing off-center on it to compensate for the differential in the length of his legs. Blance heard the story and directed Don to sit on the table. He grabbed the left foot and yanked and twisted it in what seemed like an unmerciful manner, though Don said it was painless. There was a snap-crunch that sounded awful as the foot adjusted into place. When Don stood up, it was no longer sore. Blance suggested that Don do stretching exercises to keep the bones in position, so he has taken up Yoga.

Jack's condition was more serious, in fact, the most serious of anyone in our group except for Dad. He'd been in two traffic accidents in 15 years and wanted Blance to unfuse his hip so he could get rid of that persistent limp. There was also internal infection continually draining out through the scar tissue from conventional surgery on his right side, which he therefore had to keep bandaged. Blance said he would have to get rid of the infection in order to get down to where he could work on the underlying hip bones and joint. Jack lay face up on the table, supporting himself on his elbows to enable him to watch the operation, too. Blance did not make an opening per se, but he began kneading the scars, squeezing out the pus, which stank to high heaven. As the area became liquidy, Blance scooped the gray-green goop away with his hands, occasionally rinsing his fingers in a small bowl. When the drainage became heavier, he dished it off Jack's stomach with an ordinary soup spoon, then held up the dish and spoon, grinning, and inquired of Jack, "Soup—you want some soup?" Yecch! We all groaned. It was bizarrely funny coming from the Healer. Juan informed Jack he would need several more treatments like that to clear up the source of the infection and knock it out for good. We said we would come back again.

We paid Blance in travelers checks, about 20 dollars for the two of us, a fair amount from a tourist and a pretty large amount to a Healer. There's no set fee for any operation, and the Healers rarely tell you what you owe or ask for money. It's normally by donation. But ten or twenty dollars certainly isn't out of line when a lot has been done in one session; after all, they do have to feed their families. Blance thanked us profusely, declaring that he was saving to build a chapel to work in. That seems to be the most typical goal of the Healers—or the most typical pitch!

RESULTS

We had all been affected by the morning's doings. It was only 9:30 when we left Blance's and already it had been a fantastic day. My eye was still watering, really flushing itself out at last, and Don was so happy to see me getting help that he was on the verge of tears. But Mary Ann and Nate just kept shaking their heads, speechless. Jack alone was disappointed. He had expected to hop up on someone's table and get rid of 15 years of problems in a few minutes; he'd been to two Healers so far and noticed no difference in his hip, sight or hearing. All they had done was drain away infection. We told him we thought that was pretty good, because after all, they had to start somewhere—it just doesn't work instantaneously. Nate advised him to have patience, sound advice that was a by-product of Nate's new understanding; the change in Nate was becoming more apparent. He rode back with us in Boykho's car. It was very crowded with six of us in the little Corolla, but somehow it had not seemed right to split up when we'd just experienced so much together. So Nate automatically stayed with us by unspoken agreement. I didn't really mind sitting on Don's lap on the way back!

That return trip to the hotel was the starting

point of a running joke. Both Don and Jack had had magnetic healings done on their ears, first by Virgilio, then by Blance. The Healers told them it would take time before the hearing would improve, but they were both understandably anxious. After each session, they would take off their wristwatches and listen for the tick in their bad ears. This morning, Mary Ann and I couldn't pass up the obvious one-liners. One would ask, "Hey, Jack, what time is it?" and the other reply, as if on a rehearsed cue, "He can't hear you, he's got a watch in his ear." Or one of the guys would say something like, "Damn, I've still got that ringing in my ear," and the other one would answer, "Well, pick up the phone." It was corny, silly humor, but it helped cement our friendship with the Schmidts.

There was a message at the hotel for us from Gina, the travel agent's rep: we would not be going to Baguio until the next week after all because Tony, whom we were supposed to see in Baguio, had changed his schedule. He would be in Manila this week, and would see us at the Hotel Filipinas. The new schedule was exactly what we wanted—what we had tried to tell the travel agency people the night before. We would be in Manila long enough to seek out some other Healers and to attend Sunday services at Virgilio's after all. Suddenly and coincidentally (there's that dumb word again), Tony had changed his plans—and they suited ours to the "t" without anyone having talked to him.

We were hungry, hot and thirsty. Nate went upstairs to check on Dad and the two Marges while the Schmidts and Don and I plunged into fresh fruit plates at the hotel coffee shop. For 35 cents apiece, we had mango, orange, pineapple, papaya, banana, three kinds of melon, and crackers with butter!

Jack and Mary Ann invited us over to their hotel to listen to the playback of our tape of Leonora and hear some of their other tapes. We rented a second tape recorder so we could make a dub of the interview, but it did not work, so we "borrowed" a cassette machine from a hotel employee for a modest fee. Listening to the tape of the Schmidts' medium predicting that they would meet a couple who'd lead them to the Healers, we felt very grateful to be instruments for any help they might get. A lot of people had aided us in getting ready for this trip; it seemed so right that we would be called on to pass our meager knowledge along to someone else, even that we would "coincidentally" run into them on the plane.

As we listened to the conversation with Leonora, it seemed that it had been a long time back rather than only two days ago (this was Wednesday; we had arrived and met Mrs. Pangan on Monday). It was at this moment that we got the idea of interviewing several of the Healers; we would have them tell in their own words how they work, what they believe, etc., which would be a valuable record, and effective for the people back home, either accompanying the films or by itself. We were so glad Jack and Mary Ann had brought their cassette machine. We also decided to pool our films, that is, trade copies of sequences that came out well, since they, too, were shooting Super-8's.

We wanted Nate and Dad to hear what Leonora had to say, because they seemed to be tuning in on the whole thing. We thought that the Marges (Mrs. Morton and Don's mother) had shown much less interest, probably would not understand it, and might

be peeved at being disturbed, but we didn't want
them to feel left out, either. We didn't know how we
could gracefully arrange for just the two men to hear
it. But when Don and I got back to the Filipinas,
there was no problem—as if by prearrangement, Dad
was in Nate's room having a drink, and their wives
had gone shopping.

Dad was really sunburned. We asked where he
had been. When he told us, we could hardly believe it.
The results of his healing were sure and swift, for he
and Nate had gone for a long walk and Dad, who
couldn't walk a block without taking nitro, had
walked to MacArthur Pier and back in the blazing
sun and heat! That was almost five miles round trip,
but he hadn't needed one pill, hadn't needed a nap,
and looked better than he'd looked in years. We were
almost crying, we were so happy and dumbfounded.
Dad, like Nate, was a different person; he had energy
and a hopeful outlook for the first time since I had
known him. All this was after only two treatments,
both by Virgilio, Sister Rose and their colleagues.

Boykho met Don and me for lunch. Dad and Nate
ate with their wives, the four of them seeming to
resent our not joining them. But Boykho was uncomfortable around the older couples, because they
tended to be patronizing towards him. Don's folks
did it without realizing it, I'm sure, for they were at
least polite. But Mrs. Morton seemed to distrust him.
We heard her make remarks several times about
"these foreigners" when it was we who were the
foreigners. Some of their disparaging remarks during
this lunch were directed at us in stage whis-
pers—remarks about what ingrates the young people
are these days, and who do they think they are,
ignoring their parents and friends like that. We

sluffed it off, without comment.

Friend Boykho was rapidly becoming interested in the Healers by now. He had heard of them before, and even seen one of them work when he was a child, but he hadn't had much contact with them. He was touched by our experiences so far, and full of questions and observations, which was why he had taken time away from his driving to seek us out this day. We turned the tables on him, though, plying him with questions about himself. His full name is Rotillo Kho; he calls himself Boykho because it is catchy, and also because it distinguished him from the other tourist drivers, all of whom are addressed as "Boy." That startled us, but it apparently doesn't have the connotation of a racial or class slur the way it does in the States. Boykho informed us—not quite modestly—that he had been named Driver of the Year or some such title in a government-backed contest the previous year. Then he invited us and the Schmidts to have supper with him and his family one night later in the week. We eagerly accepted on behalf of all four of us, knowing that Jack and Mary Ann would be as excited at the prospect of visiting a Philippine home as we were. We've always been of the mind that if you travel abroad but go only where other Americans go, you might as well stay home. Not many tourists in places like the Philippines have the opportunity to meet the real people, away from hotels and tourist attractions.

I had decided I wanted to buy a gold cross pendant, as an appropriate souvenir of the trip, so Don and I went shopping, up and down the streets and alleys near the hotel. We found other things: embroidered linen handkerchiefs, carved wooden dinner plates and beer mugs, some knick-knacks for a few relatives and friends. But I couldn't find a cross (I got it for my birthday a few months later instead). We were growing closer together and were getting sentimental; we'd been so spiritually uplifted by the trip to date that we decided April 4th should be a special day for us henceforth, a sort of anniversary. We took a corner table for two at dinner, and had the hotel photographer take our picture holding hands across the table. Everything was going right. It wasn't until a few hours later it went haywire.

We were supposed to have our first appointment with Tony after supper. The travel agency girl instructed us to wait in our own rooms. So we waited. And waited. We waited three hours, and shot a whole, beautiful, romantic tropical night cooped up in the room. Tony never showed up. About 9:30, we got a phone call from the travel agency telling us he would be around first thing after breakfast instead, but no explanation and no apology. We were furious.

TONY

For some reason, Don had been waking up at 4 a.m. every morning since we arrived in Manila. We wondered if someone back home was doing a telepathy experiment, but we never did find out what it was; nevertheless, he would be up, using the quiet time to meditate and pray. This morning, we ate quite early, wanting to be ready when Tony got there. Although breakfast was delicious, we did not particularly enjoy it, mainly because we were not in the mood for the company of Don's folks or the Mortons, all of whom were complaining about a lot of trivial things. Joe Bush was taking all his meals in his room, so we hadn't seen him since that first afternoon at Virgilio's.

Boykho was accompanying Mary Ann and Jack to Blance's again because, not being officially connected with our tour group, they were not included in the appointment with Tony. Don decided he would try to catch them at the Bayview and go with them. There was plenty of time before Tony was due, and we had a feeling he'd be late anyhow. So, while I waited at the Filipinas just in case Tony was on time, Don went to Blance's. He missed the Schmidts at the Bayview and had to take a cab, but it was worth his going—Blance took one of the large lumps out of the back of his neck, using Boykho's hand to make the opening.

Tony Agpaoa is the best known of the psychic surgeons, but we had heard both good and bad about him. Brent Ferre practically worshipped him, which was natural, as Tony had helped his kidney disease, and several others of our friends had seen him work either in the Philippines and/or on a visit Tony made to Chicago a few years before and thought he was fantastic. On the other hand, the Espiritista reportedly had kicked Tony out because he was getting awfully mercenary; some people said he was losing his power as a result and had been caught trying to fake openings using animal parts. We only knew a few things for certain: we had seen some pretty convincing films of his work, and he worked almost exclusively on foreign tourists, by appointment only. We were prepared to judge for ourselves, but promoter and hustler that he was reputed to be, he would have to go a long way to beat the work we'd seen Virgilio and Blance do.

Tony started off on the wrong foot, that's for sure: he was supposed to arrive right after breakfast, that is, around nine, and didn't come until almost noon. Healer or not, that is no way to treat people. We've heard it said that having to wait like that may be some kind of test of your faith in the Healer. That's ridiculous—Tony's the only one who did it to us, and besides, being plain discourteous shouldn't be a factor in spiritual tests. I was a little unsettled because Don, who was supposed to have been back by 9:00 or 10:00, was also late. The Mortons and Don's folks were waiting in the hotel room with me. Finally, there was a knock on the door. It was Tony, engulfed in a very strong vibration indeed. He looked around, consulted a list on a clipboard, and matched our names to our faces out loud, asking each of us in turn what we wanted him to work on. I studied him while he talked with the others. Nate wanted his cataracts removed. Tony nodded. Mom asked him to check her colitis. No problem, he declared. Dad said his heart was bad (not as bad as it had been, I couldn't help thinking) and Tony said okay, fine. Mrs. Morton reeled off a list of about a dozen things: migraines, high blood pressure, colitis, nervousness, and on and on; Tony looked right at her and said, just a shade sarcastically, "Mrs. Morton, have you seen a psychiatrist?" It was all I could do not to laugh. Don and I had assumed right off that most of her problems were probably emotional, not physical. Tony, at least, was very perceptive.

He was aware that I had been staring at him. He knew I was picking up a lot about him, too. He tilted his head and looked at me. It seemed he wasn't sure whether to be flirtatious, mocking, facetious, or what. Then, "Mrs. Sladek, there is nothing wrong with you." It was a flat statement, and I sensed he did not necessarily mean physically. He knew that I partially understood him and his work; I don't think he was particularly happy about it, but he had to acknowledge it. I mentioned I would like him to check my eyes, then I told him about Jack and Mary Ann and asked his permission to have them join us. He reluctantly assented, so I phoned them—half surprised to find them in their room as Don wasn't back yet—to tell them to meet us in Joe Bush's room.

Tony's assistant, a teenager named Robbie, had everything set up; one reason Tony was late getting to us is that they had already worked on Joe. (It was still inconsiderate not to let us know they were around, as we would have liked to watch, or at least be informed as to what was happening.) Robbie, at 19, had been with Tony for four years. We heard a few months after we got back from the Philippines that he finally learned how to do material healing himself. Joe's room smelled of the eucalyptus oil which Tony uses instead of baby oil or coconut oil, a sort of trademark with him.

He began to work, and personality or ego problems aside, he was truly impressive. When his power is on, it is really on. He's also quite a showman. He started with Nate, who was lying down on Joe's bed with a sheet under him. Tony placed his hands on Nate's forehead for a moment, closed his eyes, and murmured under his breath, then waved his hands in the air over Nate's head, and dropped one hand to Nate's eyes. Using only his thumb and forefinger, he gently lifted off filmy pieces of tissue, first from the right eye, then from the left: the cataracts. Nate immediately saw more clearly; when he returned to the States, his own eye doctor confirmed that the cataracts were no longer there.

Don's mother was next. It was the only operation she submitted to on the whole trip, we suppose because she was skeptical and afraid. Tony apparently inspired confidence in her because of his fame. He operated on her stomach, opening her in much the same manner as Virgilio worked, except Tony worked more slowly and precisely. First, he prayed. Then he massaged her stomach. He wiggled the fingers of his left hand around on her skin to make an opening, and leaving his left hand inside to keep it open, he used his right hand to lift the blockage which he said was causing the colitis. It was several inches long, and looked like bloody muscle.

(Mom was not watching what was happening, and was she ever startled when she saw the films of her operation!) Mrs. Morton glanced over and we couldn't believe her boorish comment—"Just like plucking a chicken!" The main difference between Tony's method and that of the other Healers is his more frequent use of tools, which he carries around in a black doctor's bag. For instance, he directed Robbie to pull the damaged tissue from Mom's abdomen with a pair of medical forceps. I was shooting movies, but I wasn't that familiar with the camera and wasn't sure if I was getting anything. I asked Tony if we could open the curtains to get more light; he shook his head, but he did move around to give me a better angle. Robbie wiped the mess off Mom's stomach with a rag and it was over. She got off the bed and continued a conversation with Marge Morton about whether the hotel beauty shop was any good. Her colitis didn't bother her much at all for a long time afterward.

I'd left the door slightly ajar, and by now the Schmidts had come in quietly. We introduced them to Tony, who did not seem overly friendly but did ask what they wanted done. Turning abruptly, he ordered Mrs. Morton to get ready to have her colitis taken care of. I took a sequence of stills, and he seemed more interested in posing for them than he did in the actual surgery, a procedure similar to what he had done on Don's mother. He was slow and deliberate to allow me to get good shots, all the while joking and talking with all of us and flirting with me.

The operation on Dad's heart was undoubtedly the most dramatic of any we witnessed on the trip; it was also one of the longest, lasting well over 10 minutes. Dad was on his back on the bed. Tony knelt beside him and went into a trance, praying half-aloud in English and Tagalog, asking for the power to be channeled through him to do God's healing work. His hands hovered over Dad's chest momentarily, then plunged in. Suddenly, he jabbed his right hand palm-up under the rib cage. When he pulled it out, he was holding Dad's heart in his hand, lifted slightly out of the chest cavity. He had used no instruments. Dad was wide awake; I asked him if he felt anything, and he said no—yet we could see his heart beating in Tony's hand. Tony called for a towel, which Robbie laid over Tony's hands. Now we couldn't see what he was doing. I shut the camera off while he worked in trance under the towel for perhaps eight minutes, then Robbie whisked the towel off at a nod from Tony. I clicked it back on. Tony was pulling goop out of the blood vessels around the heart. He dropped the stringy, whitish stuff into a pan of water, saying it was cholesterol and fat deposits. Robbie emptied the dish into the toilet.

Don had walked in just in time to see his father's heart in Tony's hand, well out of the chest. His mouth dropped open. But something terrible was happening—as soon as Don entered the room, the vibration changed; there was an instant enmity between him and Tony, partially, we're sure, because Tony was miffed at Don for not being there right from the start, and partially something much deeper, perhaps karmic in nature. Mary Ann glanced sharply at me as if to ask what had gone wrong, and Tony glared at Don even while working. I could feel Don's tension, could tell he was ready to explode. He grabbed the camera from me and roared furiously that I had forgotten to turn on the manual light meter and the films were underexposed. I didn't feel his anger was justified, but I let it ride, knowing he was just taking out something else on me. There was open hostility from several sources now, primarily between Don and Tony, but also I was angry at Don for his outburst, and the others didn't appreciate the interruption. Tony quickly finished with Dad, placing the heart gently back down in its nest, removing his hands, and massaging briefly where the opening had been. Robbie followed with a short treatment with a battery powered vibrator which Tony claimed would stimulate the circulation. Robbie cleaned up the room and packed Tony's kit. They left without working on Jack, Mary Ann, Don or me, and scarcely a word of farewell.

Things had gone smoothly up to this point of the trip, but the spell had been broken.

PUTTING IT BACK TOGETHER

Don claims he's not true to his Cancer sun sign, and he's right for the most part, but when things go wrong, he pulls into that crab shell and becomes totally uncommunicative. That's what started to happen as soon as Tony left; I did what a smart Libra should—ignored it and let Don go his own way. We had some shopping to do (still fruitlessly looking for a good jewelry store, plus picking up some more film) so Boykho drove us downtown, then showed us around Manila's Chinatown section. Don wanted to work off some of the tension, so we dropped him at a health club. Boykho told me he wanted me to meet someone special. I had no idea what he meant and he didn't explain. After a short ride, we drove up to a big gray frame house in Quezon City. It was the Khos' family home and I knew as soon as I met his parents why Boykho is so terrific.

Mrs. Kho ran outside to greet us. She's short and plump, very Spanish in appearance, and is one of those people who radiates warmth and adopts strangers—you'd have thought I was a long lost favorite cousin. She spoke very little English, but who needs language to communicate with someone you like? She served us soft drinks and cookies on the cool, stone patio. Then Mr. Kho joined us, a distinguished looking gentleman whose Chinese ancestry is evident in his features. He was friendly, too, but with a touch of oriental reserve. Boykho's brother James, age 19, was there, also; they call him either Jim or Jesse James (Boykho's an American movie buff). Unlike Boykho, James was really shy, but with that irrepressible Kho smile.

We all talked about a little of everything, and asked a great many questions about each other's countries. They were fascinated to find we'd come all that way to see the Healers. Typical urban, middle-class Filipinos, they were not well acquainted with psychic surgery. Even the ones who do know about it sometimes are hesitant to say, for fear westerners will think they are superstitious or old-fashioned or something. We got into quite a conversation on religious philosophy, so naturally the conversation turned to another tabu social topic—politics, starting with economics. I was describing a group of nice Japanese businessmen who happened to be staying at the Filipinas, whereas Mr. Kho had a very different opinion of the Japanese, stemming from his work with the anti-Japanese underground during World War II. He bears a scar perilously close to his heart from a Japanese bayonet, and Boykho recounted witnessing a Japanese atrocity when he was just a boy—they shot down in cold blood a Filipino whom they suspected was a runner with the underground. But even the Khos were forced to admit that Japanese investment in the Philippines today is a big factor in the country's economic stability, Japan being second only to the U.S. in Philippine holdings, particularly hotels and tourist spots.

The Khos approve of martial law in the Philippines, because according to them, it has made the

streets safer and cleaner. Urban Filipinos have bene-
fited from their support of President Marcos, and in
turn have nothing to fear from the regime, though
perhaps the rural and lower socio-economic groups
are in a different position; after all, it is they who
temporarily lost most of their civil rights under martial law in some parts of the country. We didn't speak
with anyone from the political opposition, or at least
no one we encountered would publicly admit to anti-
Marcos leanings.

A few years ago, some Moslems on Mindanao and
other southern islands declared they wanted a separate nation, claiming they were being discriminated
against in the predominantly and officially Catholic
Philippines. The Moslems began a guerrilla movement which seemed to be spreading until Marcos re-
instated the military government. The many peasants who were displaced by the mini-war and were
forced into shanty-towns further north near Manila
were the shame of the Philippines for a long time,
but now the government is relocating them into new
low income housing. Communist guerrillas called
Huks have been operating all over the Philippines for
decades, a la Viet Cong, and supposedly the Moslem
rebels initially had Chinese communist aid (interesting, considering that the Philippines recently has
taken cues from Uncle Sam and made overtures to
mainland China). The Philippine government tried to
play up the communist threat in order to make the
concept of martial law more palatable to the U.S.,
which gives it a lot of defense money. The Filipinos
themselves do not have a long tradition of freedom;
they've always been controlled by one dictator or
another: first, it was the Spanish, then the more
benevolent hand of the Americans, then the rapa-

cious Japanese Occupation, and finally the Americans again (still virtually in control until very recently even though the Philippines gained independence in 1946). That's why the idea of martial law or any kind of strict control doesn't bother them as much as it does us.

As I listened to the Khos, and made all these observations, the inevitable comparison to Vietnam struck me: a minority religion beginning to cry out for equality, a strong central government in complete control and getting U.S. support by saying they are fighting communism (as previously in Latin America, Greece, etc.), and evidence of the Chinese intervention. I had long deplored the Indochina situation, and the idea of my tax money holding up shaky, unpopular rightist governments in foreign countries. But the liberal rhetoric wasn't enough as I began to see the whole thing in a new light while talking to the Khos. The U.S. has a great deal at stake in the Philippines, economically, militarily and politically. Only a couple of weeks before we arrived, the American POW's from Hanoi landed in the Philippines, and considered Clark Air Force Base their first taste of freedom. The U.S. also has army and navy installations in the Philippines, because it is strategically even more important now than it was in World War II. I've seen an awful—and I do mean awful—lot of what over-Americanization can do, yet, as bad as it can be, I remain ambivalent about our presence in the Philippines. I can see both sides of the so-called "imperialist" question; the liberal philosophy appeals to me—but then I think of the many Filipinos who literally said thank you to us merely because we are Americans. And I have to respect Marcos for attempting to pull the country together and make it self-sufficient, despite disagreement with some of his harsh methods of dealing with people who oppose him.

The Khos and I moved on to more personal subjects. Mrs. Kho showed me pictures of her other children, most of whom we would be meeting later in the week, except for Boykho's oldest sister, who is married to an Australian and lives in Tokyo. I would have liked to stay longer, but Boykho wanted to beat the rush hour traffic back to the hotel. I had quite a chat with him in the car on the way back. He said he had never really had a chance to talk to an American woman alone or at great length, and had been surprised at my knowledge of politics, etc. and at my outspokenness. (His mother had said very little all afternoon.) But most of all, he couldn't get over how much Don and I trust each other, like going our separate ways that afternoon; I'm not the most liberated woman by any means, but my sense of independence astonished him. He is married and has four kids, but his family was living in the Provinces, while he found he could make more money in the city. His wife was teaching school and although he seemed proud of her, he couldn't quite like the idea of her working—a typical Filipino attitude.

I decided to take advantage of my spare time with a swim in the hotel pool. I did about 20 laps then gave up, because the pool is right next to the cocktail lounge, and the presence of a lone, tall blonde female was turning it into a fish bowl.

I went back upstairs and took stock of the souvenirs we'd bought. So far, we had some lovely embroidered hankies, and plates, beer mugs and figurines beautifully carved from Philippine mahogany (actually a variety of teak). Philippine tourist goods are unusual and inexpensive. For example, Don brought home two large wooden salad bowls that cost about $3.00 each; they'd have been ten times that at home. Also a parquet serving tray for under four dollars, ebony cane and knife inlaid with mother-of-pearl at about $3.00 apiece, and several gorgeous pieces of silver jewelry that ran around a dollar. But our pride and joy is a bas-relief wooden carving of Da Vinci's "Last Supper" at not quite $15.00. It has a special significance, being the type of thing Virgilio used to make before he was able to support himself on his donations for healing. Although ours is from a woodcarving factory in Baguio, a similar hand-finished design hangs in the hallway of his home. With all that and more, we were well under our customs limit of $100 per person duty free when we added up the receipts!

Don walked in about an hour later, still in a dreadful funk. He was mad at the world and disappointed, and I don't think I've ever seen him in a worse mood. He still had one large, hard lump on his neck the size of a golf ball, over an artery, and so far the Healers, even Blance, had only worked around it. Don, in short, was feeling sorry for himself.

Then there were the Healers themselves, who had in some ways let us down—especially Tony. I don't know exactly what we expected them to be like—perhaps something more than human, but they were only human. It had come out in our conversation with Tony that we were seeing other Healers and he was really uptight about it; we had mentioned to Blance that we would be going to Baguio, which is where Tony is from, and he asked if we would be seeing Tony. When we told him yes, he shrugged and made a face. Altogether, they were showing some negative emotions, for example, jealousy of each other; or maybe we had simply created an image of them that they couldn't possibly live up to. That was getting Don down, too. In addition, there was dissension in our own ranks. We had been going out of our way to see that the others had every opportunity to get help beyond what the tour called for. Suddenly, we were babysitters—just because we were taking some leadership in the matter of the Healers, Don was expected to take care of every little thing; we were not tour guides, but we were being taken for granted, plus, some of them were exhibiting Ugly Americanism that was difficult for us to handle. (For instance, we thought the Filipinas was a fabulous place, but a couple of the others continually griped that they'd rather be at an American hotel.)

I attempted to show Don the bright side. It wasn't easy, for I certainly understood his feelings. But after all, the trip had barely started. We would be seeing more Healers in Baguio and the Lowlands; there was time for him to get help, to get that thing removed from his neck. I told him the situation with the others was bound to improve, and at any rate, just seeing what we had so far was worth the time, effort and money. Don wasn't buying any of it.

We decided to take a walk by the harbor. It was about 9 p.m. but the park was already deserted. As we strolled along, our discussion turned into a slight altercation. Twenty four hours before, everything was perfect. Now, all of a sudden, we were taking out our mounting frustration on each other. I nearly went back to the hotel by myself because Don was anything but pleasant to be around. In fact, he came close to ordering me to go back. I wasn't keeping my cool any better, but something told me to stick it out—I figured maybe it was times like these that we needed each other most, despite our mutual sniping. We sat on the rocks at the edge of the water, saying nothing. Something odd and revolting put things back in perspective for us: rats. They were running up and down the concrete ledge a few feet below us, gnashing at each other, scavenging for food wherever they could find it—even the bodies of dead companions. Neither of us uttered a word but somehow the tension eased. We figured, okay, the hell with everybody else. If the others wanted to act like those rats, feeding off each other's negativity, let them. We would not let anybody or anything spoil what we'd worked so hard for. We would not involve ourselves in their problems; we'd just let them go their own way. If they were not willing to act at our level, then we would not let them drag us down to theirs. From now on, no more something for nothing for any of them. Maybe it was snobbish, but we felt better, albeit weary and anti-social.

Back at the hotel, a man followed us across the lobby to the elevator. We just didn't want anybody around, so instead of holding it so he could get on with us, I pushed the button and let it shut before he got to the door; it was another little thing that turned out to be significant.

BLANCE II

The next morning, we returned to Blance's—my second time, Don's third. Don's father went with us, as much for a change of company as anything else, but Jack and Mary Ann opted out. Jack was discouraged; he had not received as much help as he had hoped. He was giving Don a taste of his own medicine of the past day or so! We tried to cheer him up, but he had been let down in general, and in particular by Tony, who had been working on him at the Bayview since we introduced them. Tony, the one Healer Jack had known about all along and had real faith in, had done nothing more than Blance and Virgilio had done—clear out infection. Jack had expected much more, but he was learning that healing doesn't come easy.

Don's nose had been broken and operated on several times, and he had some trouble breathing. Blance has a reputation for handling that kind of problem which, we found, is well deserved, though his method was unorthodox, even for a Healer. He asked Don to sit in a chair as he put a piece of cotton soaked in alcohol on the end of a matchstick and shoved it up Don's nostril. Don jumped about six inches and made a face because the alcohol was burning the tender inside of the nose. After a few seconds, Blance pulled the match back out, and there was a large ball of mucus balanced on the cotton. Don sneezed and snorted for a couple of minutes, then Blance repeated the procedure on the other nostril, and again pulled out a huge wad of mucus. He said he'd actually gathered it from the sinuses, that it had not been in one piece like that originally. All Don knew was that his sinuses felt unstuffed and he was breathing more freely. The Healer took a look inside Don's ears and decided they needed to be cleaned out, too, so he put some cotton on another match, and swiped around one ear. Out came another ball of wax or something. He used the same technique to clean out Don's other ear. Blance seems to specialize in certain things like getting rid of excess garbage from the body.

Another thing we'd seen him do a lot of was removing tumors and cysts and external types of problems, so Dad asked if he could take a look at his elbow. There was a big growth of some kind which sometimes bothered him and also interfered with the mobility of the arm; the elbow was knotted and distended. Dad lay face down on the table. Blance grabbed my arm and aimed my fingers toward the swollen spot, jerking my hand downward to make the opening. Dad turned his head, looking at us in surprise! He felt the cut on his arm, and watched it slowly get longer. Juan picked up his coin, cotton and shot glass and brought the growth to a head. When he took away the glass, the arm was bleeding profusely, apparently because a lot of blood had been trapped around, in, and under the growth, like a blood blister. When it had drained away, the Healer reached into the opening and yanked out a piece of tissue that he described as the core of the lump, which he said was a non-malignant tumor. As he pulled it out, we could see the swelling go down by about 50%. Blance put a bandaid on it. It bled off and on for two or three days before closing over, eventually leaving a thin white scar about 1½ inches long; the elbow was still misshapen, but Dad had less trouble moving it.

When Don was at Blance's the day before, the Healer had told him to be sure to bring along the movie camera the next time, as he was scheduled to do an operation he thought we might want to observe. That was the understatement of the trip, for the next 20 minutes or so turned out to be a highpoint of our experience with the Healers. The patient was an elderly Filipino man. There was a large, hard tumor on the calf of his right leg, grotesque, about the size and shape of a tennis ball. It reportedly had been diagnosed by a doctor as cancerous, but the man could not afford to go to a hospital to have it taken care of.

The man's wife helped him up onto the table. She stood at the foot of the bed, right next to me. Don remained beside Blance, camera ready. Blance began probing the leg, trying to be gentle, but the area must have been very tender; the man was obviously trying not to cry out. Blance concentrated for a second. He moved to the foot of the bed and lifted my hand from my side. I felt the energy shifting from his hand to mine as he slashed my finger down through the air. A cut appeared on the tumor, which Blance inspected. He squeezed a little, and some material popped up through the surface like the head of a pimple. The Healer wasn't satisfied, so he took my hand again, and again guided it. A second slash mark appeared on the growth, a little above and parallel to the first one. I continued to hold my arm up, feeding energy to the patient, until Blance said, "Enough." My hand was shaking; I dropped it back to my side. There was almost no bleeding this time. Blance pinched the second cut, allowing a thick gray-green mass to spill out into a dish of water. It looked like an extremely large, infected pimple or sebaceous cyst and it smelled awful. Blance kept squeezing and the pasty material kept gushing out. The swelling was going down, and the skin covering the tumor was less taut, but it must have been sore, for the man squirmed and winced as Blance worked. His wife tenderly touched his ankle each time he moved, wordlessly reassuring him.

When the bulk of the goop had been squeezed out, Blance wrapped some cotton around his fingers and stuck his forefinger into the opening. He swiped around the inside of the cut, under the skin, cleaning off the inner surface. We could see his fingers twisting and tugging and pulling beneath the skin. The man was quite uncomfortable; the operation was taking much longer than most. Blance, reaching for a pair of rarely used scissors and a large tweezers, said he would have to go in after the root of the growth. For the first time, I felt myself getting queasy, and I felt faint, which had happened to me only twice before in my life. It suddenly occurred to me that it was not I who was on the verge of passing out—it was the man's wife, but I was picking it up psychically. I heard a voice that didn't belong to anyone in the room, "She needs you. You can't allow her to let him down. She needs you like he needs her." I felt better at once. There was no time or reason to analyze it. I instinctively put my arm around her thin, bony shoulder, conscious for some reason of the coarseness of her cheap cotton housedress. She was caught off guard for an instant, but acknowledged my moral support with a shy, grateful smile. I kept my arm around her while Blance dug out the rest of the root with the instruments, which were none too clean and a trifle rusty.

It was over. He put a piece of cotton over the two openings, and helped the man sit up. I suddenly realized I was weeping. The woman looked at me. She spoke no English; she didn't have to—the expression on her face was more eloquent than words could ever be, and I'll never forget it. I'd never seen her before that I am aware of and probably won't again, at least in this life, but there is a tie binding us—a tie of love, faith, and a deeply felt, shared experience. She walked out smiling, tears running down her face, her husband leaning on her for support. His leg appeared perfectly normal except for the two red lines on his calf.

Things were looking up. We had borrowed the Schmidt's tape recorder so we asked Blance for a few minutes of his time. We asked him, "How do you do the healing?" He replied simply, "I don't. God does. I am medium of the Power." He works with a spirit guide whom he suspects was a physician on the earth plane. He has to read the Bible, pray, and work at healing every single day in order to keep his gift. We asked him how he became a Healer, and between what he told us and what we had gotten from Leonora and other fairly reliable sources, we were able to piece together his story: he used to be a heavy drinker and was often on the wrong side of the law, two facts that he himself did not mention; one day—reportedly in an effort to duck a policeman, though this is also second hand information—he ran into a church where there was a spiritualist service in progress. A woman came over to him and commanded him to sit. He obeyed, his whole body shaking as the Holy Spirit entered him. He fell on the floor in a reverie, and while he was on the floor, God began to use him as a voice medium to give messages to others. Afterwards, he prayed to be able to help others and months later found he had the ability to heal. It was quite a tale, almost too melodramatic to be true.

On the way back to the hotel, we were practically high from the vibrations of the morning's activities. Blance had cleaned out my other eye and I could see more clearly than I had in years. Normally, I couldn't even read a book bare-eyed; now I was reading billboards at the side of the road without my glasses. The Healers, drawing on a common source of power, were working together to improve my vision. But that was only the beginning—a mere symbol—of our return to positivity.

Boykho pulled his car into the hotel driveway behind a taxi. A man was getting into the cab, but something made him turn around. He looked at us sharply for a split second before walking up to us. "You are the couple that's looking for the Healers. Spirit told me to find you." It was not a question, but a matter-of-fact statement followed by, "Come with me, please." We invited him into Boykho's car.

His name was Chuck Isaacs, an American who works with a Healer named Alex Orbito. We had never heard of either of them. Chuck had worked at healing all over the world, for instance, just before going to the Philippines, he studied with Harry Edwards in England. Now he was trying to learn material healing, that is, the openings, to back up his spiritual healing ability. A couple of days earlier, he had had a dream in which he'd been instructed to find an

American couple at the Filipinas Hotel: the man would have dark hair and a moustache, the woman would be blonde and taller than the man; the description was of us, of course! To top it off, he had been at the hotel looking for us the night before. He had trailed us all the way across the lobby to the elevator, but we had let it go up before he could get on. (So, that was him we had ignored. Probably a good thing—we were so negative at that point, he might have decided his dream was nuts and called the whole thing off!) What he had wanted was to ask us to meet him at 9 a.m. to go to meet Alex. "Coincidentally" that was precisely when we had driven up on our return from Blance's—such timing! Who were we to argue with Spirit or Fate or whatever? We had him give Boykho the address and off we went.

ALEX

Alex. He was a whole new ballgame as far as Healers go, and we knew it the minute we laid eyes on him for the first time, working in a tiny apartment in a poor area of Quezon City, where there were relatively few foreign tourists. He gave off that same strong vibration of healing energy, but there was another dimension to it: the subtle addition of true love and compassion that Tony lacked. Alex is the youngest of the Healers we saw—29 at the time. He is shy, and speaks less English than any of the other Healers we'd visited. His apartment was two rooms, one being a combination waiting room and workroom and the other his bedroom. About ¾ of the front room contained rows of wooden benches. Towards the rear, a square table held his guest book and absent healing list, and against the back wall were the inevitable operating table and Espiritista banner. His bedroom, a short way down the dark hallway, was sparsely furnished—just a cot, a chair, and a cross on the wall.

A couple of dozen Filipinos were sitting on the benches waiting for the day's healings to begin. An old woman began reading from a Tagalog Bible. When she had finished the passage, she came over to where we were standing, and asked us in slow, flawless English to please sign the Healer's guest book. She told us her reading had been from John: 17, which Alex always uses to open his Friday session. She herself was a volunteer assistant, whom Alex cured of cancer a few years ago, Chuck informed us as he led us back to the bedroom. On the way, we met Alex in the hall. He had been standing by his operating table when we first walked in, then he went back to the bedroom to meditate while his assistant infused the people with the proper spirit for getting help by her Bible reading and leading them in prayer. He would go to work soon.

Chuck led us back to the bedroom, though, because he wanted us to see something. There was a gnarled little native woman there, dressed in a home woven striped skirt, with a shawl over her head. Her right hand was swollen and knotted. Chuck smiled at her and took her hand. He did a spiritual healing on her, touching one hand to his forehead while he prayed and sent energy into her with his other hand. It was the "old-fashioned" laying-on-of-hands type treatment, which Chuck had been giving to her every day for several weeks. When she first came to him, she was completely crippled by arthritis all the way up that arm. After the first couple of weeks, she could use the hand, and finally her arm was almost normal, too. For some reason, Chuck said, he had always had pretty good success with arthritis (interesting, considering that arthritis is one thing the psychic surgeons do not handle very well) so he sort of specializes in cases like that, both at Alex's and in his own healing practice.

Chuck indicated the pitiful apartment. He told us Alex was saving donation money to build an indoor bathroom. What a pathetic comedown from Tony, who has become a millionaire on his earnings as a Healer, and even from Virgilio and Blance, who plan to build chapels and healing centers. Alex has moved since then, to a better place in Quezon.

We left Chuck and his patient, and went back to the main room. I wanted to get some long shots of Alex working so I sat on the last wooden bench, under the window, where the light was good, shooting some stills of Alex operating on a diabetic girl. Boykho plopped down next to me, full of information he'd garnered at Blance's that morning which he thought I would want for the book. He was snooping around and interviewing native patients for me and had a couple of interesting stories of Blance's success. He talked to the family of the man whose back Blance had worked on the first time we were there; we didn't think much about it at the time, as all he did was take a clot from the man's spine. As it turned out, the man had been going to Blance every day for five weeks, his spine so twisted that he had been in a wheelchair. Gradually, after several of Blance's treatments, he began to regain use of his legs. This morning, he had walked out on his own power for the first time, not even leaning on his son. Boykho also confirmed a story we had heard before: Blance used to work in a field or barn or wherever anyone let him or the Spirit moved him; he was hard to find without a permanent base. But an American woman whose six year old child had stomach cancer located him, and he cured the child. The mother was so grateful that she bought him the building in which he works and lives.

There was a police sergeant watching Boykho and me. He was not on duty but apparently thought this uppity Filipino was giving me, obviously an American tourist, some kind of hassle. He glared at

Boykho, and said something to him in Tagalog in a not-too-nice tone. Boykho answered him by explaining that we were together and everything was alright. The policeman wasn't too sure about it until I reassured him that Boykho was a friend of mine and there was no problem. He seemed surprised; I guess tourists don't often socialize that way with the natives (and are all the poorer for it). But he was just taking his self-assigned job seriously, protecting his friend Alex and the tourists.

Boykho went to talk to some people outside, and I moved up to the side wall for a better look at what Alex was doing. Don was already in the work area, observing from as close as possible and taking some films. A young Filipino man approached me and politely asked if I was an American and what I was doing there. He couldn't understand that an American had come all that way just to see the Healers. He thought I meant that we were in the Philippines for some other purpose and decided to check it out as an afterthought. I couldn't get through to him; he had closed his mind to the fact that any educated person could seriously study the Healers. I understood his quandary when he told me who he was—an anthropology grad student doing research for a thesis on Philippine folk arts and customs. Being educated, westernized and middle class, he was having a difficult time accepting the old, native ways. He couldn't quite understand what he had been seeing, but then, he couldn't really deny it, either. And to make matters worse, here were two perfectly sane Americans who firmly believed in this "hocus-pocus." Tourists just do not come here to see this, he said to me. I corrected him: some 300 foreigners were arriving at Manila airport daily on special tours to see them. He was aghast. He was also impressed. But all he would do is observe; he wouldn't participate or let them work on him—too subjective.

Alex's style of healing is very much like Virgilio's: a brief trance, then moving the hands quickly to make the opening and perform the operation, and finally removing the hands. He, too, rubs on oil to lubricate the skin and speed the healing, but he uses baby oil (a plain old bottle of Johnson & Johnson) because it is cheaper and less trouble to obtain. Chuck told us Alex and Virgilio used to work together, which explains the similarity in their techniques. I hadn't been paying much attention to Alex, actually, although Don had been watching for some time. I suppose I was already taking the whole thing in stride; besides, I had a different purpose to fulfill in briefing the anthro student. But suddenly the room became uncannily still. There was a shift in attention as the scattered forces of everyone in the room moved to Alex in unison. Not a word had been spoken, but there was an air of excitement as a middle-aged Filipino man jumped up on the table. Everybody seemed to sense that something unusual was about to happen. Alex pointed to the man on the table and whispered the word, "Witchcraft." I wasn't sure if I'd really heard what I thought I had heard. But apparently I had.

Don started shooting film as Alex spread baby oil on the man's stomach. He picked up a clean piece of notebook paper, holding it up to the light so we could all tell there was nothing on it, then laid the sheet of paper over the oily place on the man's skin. He closed his eyes and prayed, lips moving silently. When he picked up the paper, there were splotches on it which did not correspond to the oily spots on the skin. It looked remarkably like an x-ray. Alex pointed to an odd-shaped spot in the center of the paper. "I take out," stated the Healer. The large spot was surrounded by a series of smaller ones in a semi-circle, plus other scattered markings.

Alex ran his hands over the man's stomach. We heard a POP and it was open! Alex works very fast, but unobtrusively. There was no showboating; he was all business. Three people assisted him: the old woman, a teenaged boy, and the policeman, who tried to be helpful, but in reality was getting in both Alex's and Don's way. Alex ignored him, but Don moved around to shoot over his hands, which were blocking a clear shot of the opening. The bleeding was negligible until Alex started to bring something out of the man's stomach. The crowd gasped, us along with them. With one hand holding the wound open, Alex was gently tugging a piece of rope out of the man! Rope—about four feet of twisted hemp, covered with blood. There was no way Alex could have faked this without being caught, was there? There were too many impartial witnesses, including the skeptical anthropologist and two M.D.'s.

How could a rope have gotten there? The man couldn't possibly have swallowed it. Again Alex said, "Witchcraft." He rapidly finished the operation, removed his hands, and cleaned up the man's stomach with some moist cotton. He told the man to wait and he would show him who had cast the spell. The old woman assistant borrowed Don's ballpoint pen, and connected the dots on the "x-ray" paper; they formed a perfect outline of a woman's face, with detailed features. She held it up and showed it to the man, who nodded solemnly, obviously recognizing the face. Alex advised him to pray every night to ward off such incidents in the future. The man promised to do so, got up, and walked out. Alex, unruffled, went to work on other people after giving the x-ray with the face to Don, who absent-mindedly left it there. Boykho and I followed the patient outside, and as he spoke little English, Boykho interpreted. The man asked if we had taken pictures, obviously pleased when I told him we had; he even asked for copies. Then he asked me if I knew about witchcraft. I nodded. He seemed surprised that we had taken the whole thing so calmly (at least we appeared to). He was truly astonished to meet westerners who understood things like that, even in theory. This was the first time we had seen an apparent illustration of it, though, our past experience with so-called witchcraft having been with the neo-pagan religious aspects such as healing and white magic.

When I returned inside, Alex was getting ready to work on a more mundane problem—a chronic urinary infection that had troubled Don off and on for 12 years. Alex got rid of it for good in about 5 minutes. He had Don lie on his back on the table and loosen the waist of his slacks. He did an "x-ray" with baby oil and notebook paper on the lower abdomen, holding the results up to the camera for me. He said there was a blood clot blocking the urinary tract, the single spot that showed up on the "x-ray." Alex held his hands up in the air for a few seconds, then plunged downward into Don, his right hand appearing to go in almost wrist-deep. The pressure of the opening caused a spurt of blood that rained on those of us standing nearby. It miraculously missed the camera, but I did have blood spots on my clothes and shoes. Don wasn't paying much attention to Alex. He was too busy playing cinematographer, giving me directions on how to use the camera. (And the films did turn out.) Alex reached into the opening with his free hand, and pulled out a large clot, and dumped it into a dish of water so I could get a picture of it. He wiped up with some dry cotton, took away his hands, and that was that. Don sat up and waved at the camera, grinning and talking to show he was awake. He'd gone to several doctors and gotten antibiotics whenever that infection cropped up, or taken lots of vitamin C to help control it. But neither he nor the doctors could cure it; the problem has not recurred at all since we came back from the Philippines.

The old woman was prepping people for the psychic surgery by giving them spiritual injections, similar to what Virgilio had done with the imaginary hypodermic. But it felt different when she did it, in the crook of the arm. With Virgilio, I had felt the energy flowing into me when he pushed the plunger of the invisible hypo. When this woman gave me a spiritual injection, it felt more like the jab of a needle, followed by an electric-like shock running up my arm.

There was no doubt about it, Alex was the best Healer we had seen, either in person or on someone's films. Not only his healing ability, but his whole attitude was so beautiful! In addition, there was some kind of karmic tie between Alex and Don which also included Boykho, strong enough that even he, who'd never claimed psychic sensitivity, was picking up on it. We just knew we would all be good friends. We couldn't get over the fact that if it hadn't been for Tony's "accidental" change of plans, and our "just happening" to run into Chuck that morning, we'd have already been in Baguio and not even met Alex. Alex would be having his next full-scale services, with voice mediums and all, at 3 p.m. the next day, Saturday. He issued us a special invitation and we promised to make every effort to be there. We also made an appointment for Chuck and Alex to come to the hotel Sunday morning. We had every intention of making it back to Alex's before Sunday; it would have to be really something to keep us away. It was.

MORE WITH TONY

Tony had scheduled another consultation with our group in the afternoon, so we all waited for him in Joe Bush's room. It was very quiet; we were all wrapped in our own thoughts. Despite the high level of the morning at Alex's, Don had a headache. I did a quick energy healing on him and it seemed to help. I used the hiatus to update my journal.

We had reached one conclusion: Spirit was certainly guiding this whole trip, at least as far as Don and I were concerned. There just couldn't be so many coincidences! But the Healers had been a disappointment in some ways. Alex came closest to what we had expected—honest, sincere, devoted, and spiritual; he didn't seem to be jealous of the others or have any ulterior motives, and he wasn't on an ego trip like Tony. We told the rest of the group all about Alex (well, not all—they would not have dug that rope thing at all) and invited them to see him Sunday after he was through with us.

Another thing we had observed is that the Healers are very sex role oriented. Every one of them had commented on my height, perhaps because in the Philippines, even more than at home, women are ordinarily quite small and rarely are taller than their men. The Healers couldn't figure us out. They all asked if Don and I were brother and sister; I thought maybe they were picking up something between us from a past life, but I don't really feel it. They were also very sympathetic when we told them that we did not have any children, patting me on the shoulder and saying "Oh, too bad, what a shame." It didn't seem to occur to them that we wanted it that way. The Philippines is, after all, still a most Catholic country, even for those who have broken away from the Church.

Things seemed to be better this time when Tony came in. He did a magnetic healing on my eyes, and even worked a little on Don, taking some clots out from behind his ears. From then on, he pretty much ignored Don except to fully cooperate in getting better angles for the films. What a publicity hound! He preened and posed for both our shots, joking and flirting with me while I took stills.

He worked a lot more on Joe. Tony's theory was that the motor ataxia was partially caused by blood clots putting pressure on the brain. He directed Joe to sit in an armchair with a towel draped around his neck and shoulders. Leaning on his cane, Joe painfully made his way over to the chair, where Tony prayed over him for a minute. He rubbed the top of Joe's head; the skin split open and Joe had to blink a droplet of blood away from his eye. As Tony worked, we could actually see down to Joe's skull. Tony was really "on" and it seemed he wanted to make sure we knew how well the Power was coming through. We couldn't blame him, with so many stories circulating that he is losing his ability. But regardless of what tricks he may have pulled before or since, it was working this day, and to prove it, Tony pulled the skin back and held it open for the camera so Don and

I could each get clear shots of the opening. Tony directed Robbie to pull out a couple of clots with the forceps, while Tony used his hands to hold the head open. Joe was wide awake and talking with us through the whole thing; in fact, he was watching it by holding up Marge Morton's compact! Robbie was assisting, and doing his best to keep the blood from dripping down Joe's face. Unfortunately, Robbie got in the way of the cameras a few times, a mistake Tony never makes. When they were done, Tony folded the skin back into place to cover the opening, jerked his hands away, and every trace of the operation disappeared.

Joe had to lean on his cane to get even as far as the bed, but he said he was beginning to feel better; he wasn't losing control of his muscles or his temper so often, following a series of treatments from Tony in addition to what Virgilio had done the first day. Tony continued to work on him, this time removing clots from the top of the spine, with Joe face down on the bed. Tony made an opening at the base of the neck. He said he was really gathering excess blood from several places along the spine into clots, but he only needed one opening to bring them out, which was in keeping with what Blance had been telling us about the stuff he takes out of people. Again, Tony pulled the skin back away from the opening for our cameras, allowing Don to open the drapes this time, so there was better light than the other day. We were surprised at how little bleeding there was when Tony worked, even on the head. He said he does it on purpose—that his magnetic power causes the blood to clot so he can work better. That didn't quite fit in with what we had observed—what we'd noticed was a less than normal bleeding anywhere near the Healers' openings; he was talking about it clotting behind the openings or at their edges. We didn't know if he works that differently, if he was trying to impress us, or if he knew something about how the Power works that the other Healers didn't know. Or maybe it was a matter of simple semantics.

Tony pointed to Dad and asked him to lie down on the bed face down. He took my hand and ran it over a spot on Dad's lower back. "Do you feel the lump?" he asked me; I did indeed. He said it was foreign matter—perhaps a calcium deposit—that didn't belong there. He made an opening almost effortlessly, without trance or additional prayer, just by wiggling his fingers over the spot. The skin split open and Tony took out a hunk of pinkish tissue of some sort. Robbie swiped a rag over Dad's back and of course, there was no sign of any operation. "Feel again, Mrs. Sladek." I put my hand where Tony had done his thing: there was nothing out of order now; the back was smooth and soft.

After each operation, Robbie ran the battery powered massager over the area Tony had worked on. Tony again stated the electricity and massage were to stimulate the nerves and circulation, no big revelation. Before he left, he handed Mrs. Morton a bottle of pills which he claimed would help her body regain its balance of natural forces. I read the label—some type of homeopathic formula, maybe vitamins or minerals, or perhaps just placebos. It was one of the rare times when we saw or heard of a Healer prescribing anything, aside from suggesting changes in diet occasionally.

Tony is an excellent technician, one of the best when the Power is working strongly through him. He's also got showmanship, which can be an asset when it comes to proving his healing ability to skeptics, and his education and relative sophistication may be important for communicating with a lot of westernized people. But something is missing, the Spanish word "simpatico" probably coming closest to what it is. It doesn't translate well, but is sort of an elusive sense of empathy, a sensitivity to other people that makes you really care for them. His lack of this intangible quality showed itself in a general lack of consideration: he stopped working when we ran out of film; he stood us up several times; he promised to come back that very evening, for example, but instead he sent Robbie around to the rooms with envelopes for donations. He also expects substantially more money than the other Healers.

The west coast travel agent who had set up our tour was in Manila leading a tour of fellow travel agents. He and Don started talking after supper that evening, as he'd never before handled a tour to the Healers and was getting very interested in the whole thing. He was considering arranging tours that would include several Healers, because Don had told him that ours, which officially included only Tony, was less than satisfactory. He was so psyched that he talked to a friend of his who knew more about the Healers; the friend sent us a copy of one of Tony's books, and also the name of a woman who was reputed to be a tremendous Healer. She worked only on weekends, so we braced ourselves for a hectic Saturday—Blance, then Tony, followed by this Mrs. Dimapilis (whom we had never heard of), and finally the weekly church service at Alex's.

BLANCE AGAIN AND ALMOST TONY

Don and I got up at 5 a.m., ate, and arrived at Blance's about 7:00. He took more deposits out of Don's nose and neck, then did a massage healing on a varicose vein on Don's leg; we watched it straighten out even as he worked on it. He advised Don to massage it a little every day to keep it from curling up again.

We didn't stay very long because we wanted to be back and waiting when Tony arrived. There was enough tension with him already, without our walking in late, and although he wasn't our favorite Healer, he was helping the others a lot. There was no point in aggravating the situation with either him or them. We'd taken a cab to Blance's, and wouldn't you know it—now that we were in a hurry, we couldn't find one to take us back to the hotel. Don asked a traffic officer at a nearby market where we could get transportation to Hotel Row. The cop must have thought he was nuts, a tourist in that native neighborhood at morning rush hour. Nevertheless, he told Don our best bet would be the jeepneys; the only other thing that seemed to be around was the two-person horse carts. (They are the least expensive public vehicles, and little wonder: they're like a high rickshaw, and terribly wobbly, with the horse hitched so that its hind feet are bound to a stick—otherwise, the buggy would rear-end the horse and tip over. The horses had a most unusual gait!)

We finally flagged a jeepney, without really having any idea of where it would take us. It was better than just standing there on the corner. Besides, it was even more fun this time than it had been with Leonora. The workers who were our fellow passengers couldn't believe we were there at all, and the driver of the pink and yellow striped minibus actually stopped it so we could hop on—they usually only slow down, and you jump on at a run. The people moved over to make room for us and a man got up to give me a seat. We zigzagged around Rizal Province into the industrial area in Makati, its largest town. The jeep turned in and out of the driveways of factories and office buildings letting people off. We finally saw some plants that we recognized from the rides out to Blance's: Dodge trucks, Upjohn, the telephone company (a beautiful modern building nationalized by the government, along with the rest of the communications industry). We got off on the main highway as soon as we spotted a cab coming up behind the jeepney.

Robbie had instructed all of us to wait in our own rooms for the Saturday morning session with Tony. Tony wasn't there when we got back to the hotel at 9:00, so we called Joe Bush. Joe hadn't seen him either, but did promise to give us a buzz if and when he heard anything; we promised to do the same. At 11:00, we decided we could find better things to do than waste half a day waiting for Tony again. We left the room and were assailed by the odor of eucalyptus. He was surely somewhere in the hotel, then. We knocked on Joe's door, which was unlatched, and he called to us to come in. Our whole group was sitting there—Joe, Don's folks, and the Mortons. Don's mother asked, "Where have you been? Tony has been and gone. He's through with us." I have never before or since been so completely possessed by anger. Don, who ordinarily is very cool when angry, was doing a not-so-slow boil. Speaking of being through with people! We let them all have it, both barrels. Not one of them had thought to let us know Tony had arrived, yet we had made it possible for them to see Virgilio, Blance, and Alex, we had fielded all their petty complaints with the travel agent, etc. And Joe had given his word he would let us know if he heard from Tony, less than two hours before! Even Don's parents had not had the decency to try to find us. His mother supposedly had knocked on our door and gotten no answer. She said she must have gone to the wrong room, and that was even dumber, because we'd been there nearly a week and all our rooms were together. She made matters even worse when, in an effort to soothe us, she mentioned that Tony had asked where the people with the cameras were.

We couldn't take any more. We stormed out, slamming the door. From now on, they could go their own selfish way. We were so furious, we weren't even watching where we were going. Getting off the elevator, we literally ran into Tony, who asked where we had been. And we told him—waiting in our room, per your instructions. Neither he nor anyone else had informed us of what was happening. We secretly wondered if Tony had planned it on purpose on account of the bad vibes between him and Don, but he apologized and was really very nice about the whole thing. At least we got it off our chests. And giving credit where credit is due, there is a calming air about him; we felt better after talking with him. He was on his way to work on the Schmidts and others at the Bayview.

We bumped into Chuck Isaacs in the lobby. By the time we had chatted a bit with him, we had cooled off considerably, but we had not changed our minds about Tony or our so-called friends and relatives. And that was our state of mind when we set off for what turned out to be the most fantastic episode of the trip.

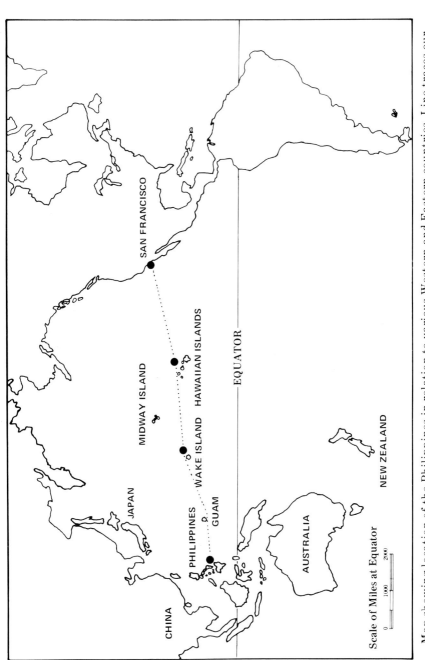

Map showing location of the Philippines in relation to various Western and Eastern countries. Line traces our route from the west coast of the U.S. to Manila, a distance of about 8000 miles.

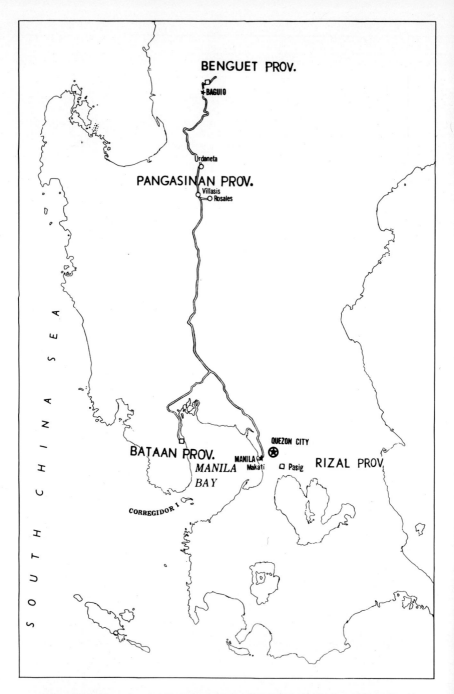

Points of interest in the Philippines relating to this book, centering on the Provinces of Manila, Rizal, Pangasinan and Benguet on the main island, Luzon or Lujon.

Early morning over the Philippines, flying into Manila through volcanic mountains to Luzon.

Traffic jam, Manila-style—and it's not even rush hour; note the variety of vehicles in this native shopping district.

A Manila street with billboards advertising a very popular pastime, moviegoing. Bottom one is for a martial arts film, a few months ahead of the fad in the United States.

Patrol girls try—unsuccessfully— to ignore our cameras outside the school where Leonora Pangan works.

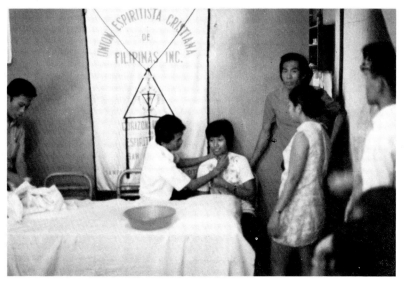

Alex Orbito does a magnetic healing on a girl who has diabetes. Not all healings require an opening, or even lying on the table. The Espiritista banner of Alex's "Center" hangs in the background.

The Quezon City apartment complex where Alex lived and worked in 1973; now, he works in a different apartment there but lives away from his Center.

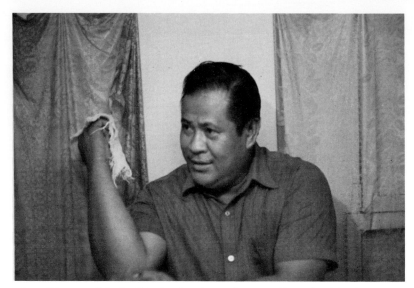

Juan Blance of Pasig, Rizal, who always has a smile and a joke for the people he heals. Here, he cleans up between operations.

Horse cart parked in front of "Suburban Hardware" in Pasig; "plumbing" is misspelled on the sign. A jeans store and jeep parts shop are next door. In the lower right hand corner, Don (striped shirt) asks directions from a traffic officer.

Boykho, Don's father and Don in the waiting room at Blance's, sitting under a Disney poster, early in the morning.

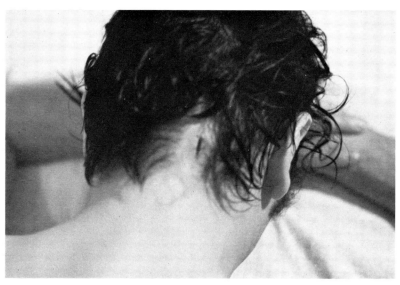

Blance is one of the few Healers who leaves a mark, which then closes by itself and becomes a small scar. The opening on Don's neck was deep when Blance removed a cyst next to an artery, but there was hardly any bleeding.

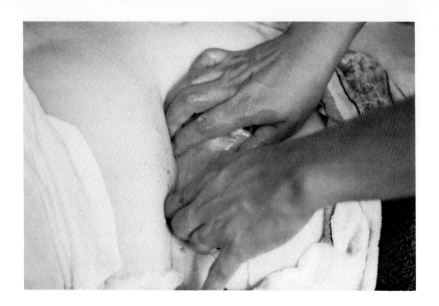

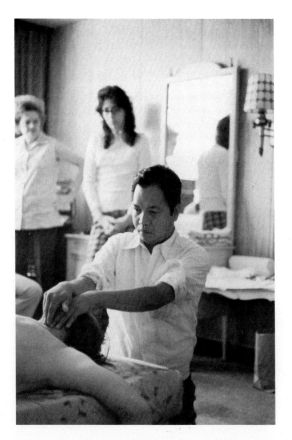

Tony Agpaoa at work, clockwise from lower left.

(1) Typical preparation as he prays over Joe Bush prior to opening his neck.

(2) Making an opening on Marge Morton's abdomen.

(3) With Robbie's assistance, Tony removes blockage he said was causing her colitis.

(4) Finally, the body has closed, and Robbie cleans up the little bit of blood.

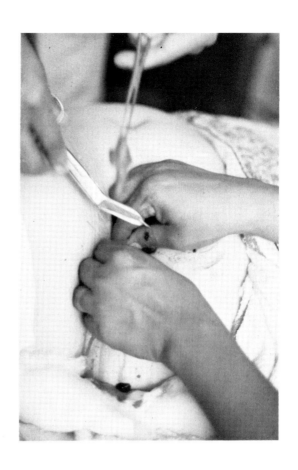

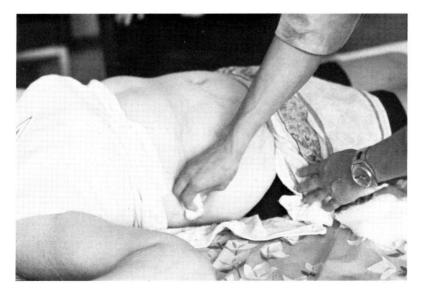

(Top) Virgilio Gutierrez helps Mary Ann Schmidt in developing her own "Spirit Gift" with an energy transfer. Sister Rose, former pharmacist, stands behind Mary Ann with Virgilio's younger brother.

(Bottom) Duplicate crucifix to the one at Mrs. D.'s set up in an apartment in Makati. It was later moved to the rooftop for the Novena service we attended.

(Top) Homes dot the hillside behind Tony's house on the edge of Baguio City.

(Bottom) A policeman directs traffic at the major crossroads in Urdaneta, one of Pangasinan Province's larger towns.

En route from Manila to Baguio, the scenery consists of distant volcanos, sugar cane fields, rice paddies, and much more. This is near Clark Air Force Base.

A not uncommon scene in the rural Philippines: boys riding a water buffalo and a man carting goods to market down a side road in Pangasinan.

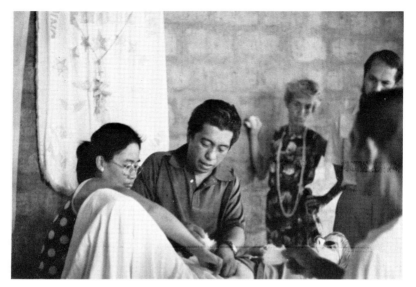

Jose Mercado works on a tourist at this chapel in the lowlands, as other Americans look on. The chapel is a plain, concrete block building. Each Healer has an individual design for the Espiritista banner.

A one family house in a lowland village, built up on stilts for protection from flooding in rainy season. Children play under the house, while chickens and animals share the yard.

(Top) The marketplace in Urdaneta, where lowland farmers sell their produce, and buy anything from food and clothing to housewares and bolo knives, like a huge flea market.

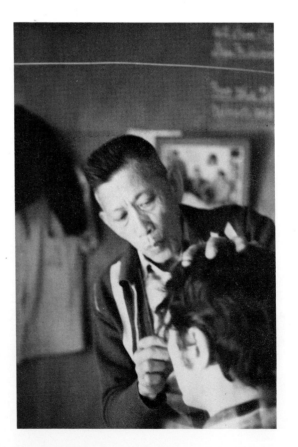

(Bottom) The senior member and founder of the Espiritista, Euleterio Terte, works on Don at his home in Baguio.

(Top) Josefina Escandor-Sison in the doorway of her thatch home in Villasis, Carmen-Rosales, Pangasinan.

(Bottom) Children play in front of the concrete block schoolhouse, which doesn't look much different from surrounding homes in Rosales.

(Top) Not an ancient wargod of a Philippine tribe, though you might think so as you head toward it down the mountainous road from Baguio; it's the Lions Club War Memorial, carved from a single hunk of granite. Immensity is demonstrated by the motorcyclist on the highway in lower right corner.

(Bottom) Marcello Jainar does a magnetic healing on Don's ears, working in a relaxed, casual manner in the front room of Tony Agpaoa's in Baguio.

MRS. D.

We got a cab driver who assured us he knew
exactly where this Mrs. Dimapilis lived when we
showed him the address and gave him approximate
directions. He misled us, for he got as far as Makati,
but could not find the street. We left his cab and got
a local one, with no better luck—the driver stopped
three different policemen to ask where it was, but
none of them knew. It was turning into One of Those
Days, with this thing looking more and more like a
wild goose chase. We were tired, angry, and discouraged; it was as if we had to overcome a regular obstacle course to find this woman. Was it some kind of
a test of our persistence or determination or sincerity? At last, after again stopping to ask, the driver
was able to locate the street. And no wonder we had
had trouble: this was a very good neighborhood, but
the street was hardly more than an alley. After all
that searching, we ended up only two blocks off Rizal
Blvd., the main street in Makati.

These people were obviously well-to-do. The
house was the nicest we had seen in the Philippines
to date, large, green stucco, with a good-sized garden
and a breezeway in front. On the breezeway were
some padded lawn benches, so we sat, joining a dozen
or so Filipinos who were also waiting to see Mrs. D.

For the most part, they were a bit better dressed than the patients at Blance's and Virgilio's, and they all spoke good English. As usual, they couldn't get over our coming all the way from the States to see the Healers. I was seated next to a young mother whose baby had a bad cold. She was bringing her to Mrs. Dimapilis rather than going to a doctor. That baby had a thing for my purse—just loved the taste of the red canvas strap, and I enjoyed playing with the child. Come to think of it, we were getting hungry, too. We'd rushed out without thinking about lunch, and hadn't eaten since 8:30 that morning. (It was nearly 1:00 now.) There was a little thatched store of sorts on the corner about a half block away, so Don went to see what he could rustle up for us. Some snack—a few small bananas, a bottle of warm Sprite and some pre-packaged brownies. Not exactly in keeping with our high protein, mostly organic diet, but beggars can't be choosers!

Every once in a while, the front door of the house would open and someone would come out. One of them was a teenaged boy. The woman next to me, a neighbor of the Dimapilises, said he'd been in a wheelchair until recently, and was walking now because of Mrs. D. The waiting crowd was mixed as far as age, etc. There were two attractive young women sitting in garden chairs opposite us who smiled and said hello. We'd been sitting there almost an hour when a pretty teenaged girl came out of the house and began to hand out numbers. We could feel something special was going on inside. The girl went back in, then came out in a few minutes. She addressed Don and me, "Come in. We were expecting you. We didn't know you were here yet," which was a shocker, because we hadn't told anyone we were coming. She introduced herself as Dinah Camano, Mrs. Dimapilis' niece. We followed her through the door into a living room well-furnished and packed with people; everybody but us was Filipino. A tiny woman of about 50 approached us. We knew instinctively that this had to be Mrs. D. She said, "I know why you are here. You want to write a book." Glancing at the camera slung over my shoulder, "You can't take any pictures, but I'll help you with it." Well, we hadn't mentioned to anyone outside of our tour group—even the travel agent—about the plans for a book, but as if that wasn't enough to astound us, she continued, "And you come for help. You (looking at me) for your eyes, and you (to Don) for your ears." There was just no way she could have been told these things because we didn't even have any mutual acquaintances who knew.

The crowd parted and made room for us on a sofa. Just then, a crippled man left the house in a wheelchair. He'd been coming to Mrs. D. for several weekends in a row, confident of her promise that she could help him to walk again. His young son said the man was getting feeling and movement in his legs for the first time. It would take a while, they realized, but the whole family felt sure their husband and father would eventually walk out that door.

The two young women who had spoken to us in the garden were the next people to be invited in. They sat next to us, and one of them treated me like we were old friends, dumping her problems on me (a common phenomenon among Libras, I'm told, to have strangers crying on your shoulder). There was something wrong with her eyes; whenever she drove anywhere, her vision would cloud and force her to pull off the road. So the other girl, who was her cousin, brought her to see Mrs. D., who lived near them.

Mrs. D. was standing in front of a girl about 15 years old who was seated on the other sofa. All around the girl, people were praying and manipulating rosaries. The atmosphere was heavy and positive, but in a different way than we had encountered at the other Healers' places. The room seemed to buzz with spiritual power and energy, much more charged than the comparatively casual, relaxed air of the other Healers. We didn't know what was wrong with the girl, but she was obviously frightened. We couldn't hear what Mrs. D. was saying, but we did hear an excited whisper as a single word circulated around the room—"Exorcism." The air became tense. A man was holding the girl down on the couch, steadying her with a hand on her shoulder. However, Dinah told us nothing much would be happening for a while. She led us into the dining room, where someone had fixed us a plate of rice cakes and Filipino coffee. I was hungry, yet didn't want to miss anything. We nibbled at the food, which, like the native coffee, was a little too sweet for our taste.

I snuck back into the front room just in time to be very shaken by what I saw: the girl was floating several inches above the couch! Mrs. D. commanded her down and she fell sharply to the seat, gasping for breath. She was crying, but put her hand to her throat and said the pain was gone. Don, who had been standing in line to get into the john, came back in just at that moment, having missed the levitation by only a few seconds. He was disappointed, but it had occurred too fast for me to call him. It certainly had not been a trick for our benefit; we were not supposed to have seen it at all. In fact, Dinah immediately asked us to go back and finish eating. We were much too excited, and also puzzled about the apparent attempt to keep us away.

When we returned to the living room again, Mrs. D. was working on Rose, the young woman I'd been talking with earlier. Mrs. D. was having no luck with what she described as an "evil spirit" that was causing the eye trouble. Rose was visibly upset, which was making it more difficult for Mrs. D. to concentrate on her healing prayers. She asked Rose to come back again the next day, after mass. Rose sat beside me again, asking me over and over if I saw something evil about her. What could I say? I was over my head just trying to take in everything that was going on. I certainly couldn't make any judgements about spirits or alleged causes of somebody else's afflictions. I tried to comfort her as best I could, but I was almost as confused as she was.

Suddenly, Mrs. D. was in front of us, and the chain of events that followed isn't totally clear even now. She asked us if we were Catholic. We told her no. (Don had been raised Catholic but left the church years ago, and I'm a renegade protestant.) I half expected the kind of reaction I used to get in Mexico when folks found out I wasn't Catholic—"Oh, that's too bad," implying they were sorry I would have to go to Hell. But Mrs. D. wasn't like that; she just asked if we believed in God. We told her that we did, and were becoming more faithful every day on this trip, which seemed to satisfy her. She informed us that she can heal only people who have faith of some kind, regardless of what religion they are. Then she left us sitting on the couch, while she took a dozen or so people upstairs with her for a few minutes. When she came back down, she was ready to tell us her own story.

The very first revelation about herself shocked

us: she is fatally ill. Being a devout Catholic, the first thing she did when the doctor told her she was dying was to pray before her bedroom crucifix. She became enraptured and had a vision. Ever since then, she has been able to heal people. She does no openings, and she works only on weekends, aided by her husband and some friends and neighbors. During the week, she is too weak to do anything, but she's such a powerhouse on weekends that she has become the major spiritual leader in the neighborhood. Church officials aren't too happy with her, because she's often more influential than they are, yet she remains a devout Catholic. She simply feels that she has a mission to fulfill before she passes, and that the Church's attitude should have no bearing on it. The people love her, affectionately addressing her as "Tita (Aunt) Ester."

She showed us a heavily perfumed, red velvet cloth which she said was the breechcloth from her crucifix. She put it to my face and ordered me to kiss it and breathe deeply. I was out like a light, in deep trance. I've been in trance many times before and since, both meditative and hypnotic, sometimes so far gone that I speak languages I do not know in this life. But I've never experienced one quite like this; I was totally relaxed, but fully cognizant of the situation. I did not feel as though I had been drugged or anything. Mrs. D.'s voice filtered through to my subconscious. She touched me gently, moving her hands over my head and eyes. I was drifting in and out very comfortably, barely aware of other people. She moved over to Don, who was seated next to me, and began stroking his head. As she did, he, too, went into a heavy trance. She ordered me to watch her closely, so I forced myself to pay attention while she worked on Don. She told me I would have to perform exactly the same procedure on him the next three times he got one of his bad headaches. After that, she said, his hearing would return to normal. (I must have missed something she did because it didn't work out exactly that way.)

First, she put a dish towel soaked in hot water around his head, turban style. The water had to be as hot as he could stand it, and contain precisely three grains of salt. She massaged his ears, rotating her hands in a clockwise motion from the cheeks to the back of the neck. While she worked, sweat poured off her; her husband kept wiping her back under her blouse with a towel. Don was hardly aware of anything at all, he, too, drifting lazily in and out of trance, not paying any attention to anything physical. But his headaches have practically disappeared and he could hear a little better for a while—who knows how much Mrs. D. had to do with it?

It was 2:45 p.m. Don wanted to get to Alex's for services at 3:00 and was going to be a little late. I told him I wanted to stay and would see him back at the hotel for dinner. It was unusual for us to split up like that, but we each felt compelled to go our separate ways. I wanted to see Alex again, too, but the whole vibration of Mrs. D.'s was getting to me. I just couldn't bring myself to go. Don left. Mrs. D. didn't seem upset about it, nor were we upset with each other. I closed my eyes and impulsively began reciting the Lord's Prayer under my breath. I hadn't prayed like that in years, and I was really hearing the words and feeling what they meant for the first time, not just repeating them by rote. I opened my eyes just in time to see Don come back in through the front door. He told me later that he had gotten as far as the corner when it dawned on him how fantastic things were at Mrs. D.'s, and how much he was remaining under her "spell" even out of the house, so he turned around and came back, and found Dinah waiting for him at the door. He couldn't quite figure out why he had left in the first place.

Mrs. D. was standing before us again. I felt hot then cold, which often happens to me in the midst of a psychic experience. Then there was no physical sensation at all, because more than likely I was out of my body, the way Don had been that first day at Virgilio's. I looked down and saw everyone in the room kneel in front of where we were sitting on the couch; I saw the physical me still sitting there, the body's eyes closed. There were about 30 people there, saying the Lord's Prayer in Tagalog. I do not speak it, nevertheless, I understood their words without having been told what they were saying. Mrs. D. began to speak in a low voice of the marvelous powers of Christ and God, as I slipped back into my body, swaying slightly. She asked me to take her right hand and Don to take her left, and ordered him to squeeze as hard as he could. He's very strong, but couldn't even move it. Her voice took on a deeper, more commanding timbre. And she asked, "Are these the hands of a dying woman?" For an instant, they were—soft and white and weak and small, but before I could utter a sound, they seemed to change. The grip was so tight I could not move my hand. I opened my eyes and saw Mrs. D. standing alone in front of us, but the hands appeared large and brown and calloused. "What hands are these?" demanded the voice. I spoke through tears, "The Hands of the Lord." Don echoed me, also sobbing. I knew it was me who had spoken, and yet it seemed like someone distant. And as quickly as it started, it ended. I had recently read Brad Steiger's classic book *Revelation: the Divine Fire*. What we had just experienced was similar to accounts he had reported of various people's alleged contacts with God, etc. It seemed pretty farfetched when I read about it; it does now when I write about it. But it did happen. And there was more.

When we were fully awake, Mrs. D. asked us to follow her to the window. She stood in the light and asked us to look into her eyes and describe what we saw. I gazed into her pupils. She said, "Do you see them, do you see the crucifixes?" I sure did—it was not merely crosses of reflected light; in each eye was a perfect miniature crucifix complete with the body of Christ. Don heard and saw it differently: he heard her ask if he saw a cross, and responded yes. Dinah took us upstairs to see the famous crucifix from which Mrs. D. received her Gift. It looked like many others we had seen: about two feet high, of wood, with the Christ figure in marvelous detail in plaster, wearing a cloth identical to the one Dinah was putting away. From that room Dinah led us down the stairs and out of the house. Mr. and Mrs. D. were in the garden; Mrs. D. smiled and asked us if we had understood everything she had said today. I told her we did not speak Tagalog, but even the parts that were not in English we understood "here" (tapping my heart with my fist). She smiled again, nodded and invited us to return Monday evening for a special Easter ceremony. We were elated at the thought of coming back again. Dinah handed us each a spray of sampaguita, (aha! That was the aroma we had smelled on the breechcloth; although I hadn't been able to place it previously, it's impossible not to recall its distinctive scent) and Mrs. D. gave us a jar of coconut oil with dried sampaguita blossoms floating in it. Don offered her a donation, which she politely refused, explaining that she never takes money for her healing.

Dinah, Rose, and Rose's cousin Gina wanted to take us somewhere else. We walked about three blocks to a large, rich looking home that Dinah said belonged to a politician. In the garage was a sort of chapel, with a crucifix identical to the one at Mrs. D.'s. The reason for its being there? Mrs. D. had cured the man's son of polio and he had set it up at her request, in payment. The three young women kissed the feet of the Christ figure, and wiped the brow with a handkerchief. It seemed like a hollow ritual to us, but we followed suit, not wishing to offend them. I noted with some surprise that the statue was already wet again, although it was free-standing and didn't have any visible wires or tubes or vials near it. Dinah told us this Christ and others like it often drip real sweat and blood, especially on Good Friday. We'd heard tales of such things—it sounded impossible, but then, much of what we had experienced on this trip so far was "impossible!"

Next, they took us to an apartment building a couple of blocks away. We walked up two flights of steps to a third floor apartment in which another altar was set up. We all went through the motions of kissing and mopping the Corpus Christi. I'd brought my camera that day with only one shot left on the roll, and this was where I took it; that shot of the altar and crucifix is the only souvenir we have from that memorable day.

On the way to the cabstand, we asked Dinah what she had meant when she had said Mrs. D. was expecting us. She told us her aunt had a dream a few nights before in which she was advised what to do with an American couple who would be over on Saturday. That was two days before the travel agent had even gotten her name from his friend! That is why we were welcomed—they knew through Spirit that we were sincere, were ready for such a heady experience, in short, were meant to be there. The evening would be a letdown. No matter how much we wanted to, we could never fully share that day with anyone, could never communicate completely what had gone on. We don't talk about it too often, and when we do, such as in this book, all we can do is relate it without offering explanations. We only know that Mrs. D. profoundly affected us.

HASSLE

While we were having our religious experience, Jack and Mary Ann were hassling with Diplomat Travel, trying to gear their plans to ours so we could stay together. Our tour group was scheduled to fly to Baguio on Monday, but we and the Schmidts decided to hire Boykho to drive us up Tuesday instead so we could see more of the countryside and the Manila area Healers. (We had never heard of Mrs. D. when we set up our plans this way, but with this schedule we were able to accept her invitation for Monday night. Coincidence?)

This was Saturday evening. Jack and Mary Ann had asked the Bayview for their hotel bill so they could get their finances straight before checkout on Tuesday. The bill was atrocious, substantially more than the $15 or so per night they were supposed to be paying. They traced down the extra cost: Tony, who had worked on them a few times after we introduced them, had informed the Bayview that the Schmidts were on a Diplomat tour. Without consulting them, the management was charging them a tour price without its advantages—for example, they were paying for their own meals despite the fact the tour cost included breakfast and dinner. They were understandably upset and came to Don with the problem. Don was livid. He left messages for our travel agent and for the head of Diplomat. He was getting nowhere. Jack was becoming despondent, and Mary Ann was mad at Jack for letting Don fight their battles for them. We didn't mind in this case; it was just that we were still "high" from the afternoon with Mrs. D. and weren't functioning too well on business matters. In the end, it was Boykho who came to the rescue. He lectured Jack, telling him to quit feeling sorry for himself and try a little love and patience. It was nice of Boykho to concern himself, when he could have been out making money driving other tourists around. It was also amusing and gratifying; he'd scarcely heard of the Healers a week before, and here he was taking matters into his own hands. He even gave us the name of a high government official his brother knows, whom we could call to report Diplomat's behavior.

Eventually, it was straightened out without resorting to getting anybody in trouble with the government. Don finally got through to the head of Diplomat, and politely told her off, also telling her how incompetent her assistant had been so far. She put things right with the Bayview, got the overpayment back, and in general was very professional.

BOYKHO AND BLANCE

Boykho was practically one of the family by now. He always seemed to turn up when we needed him, for driving, translation, questions. He seemed to like being around us. It wasn't just the money he was making; he often stayed just to talk with us, even when we told him he was free to take other passengers. We loved listening to him. He had new angles on everything, and we were fascinated by his staccato, accented English, laced with outdated slang terms he'd picked up from American servicemen. His favorite expression was, "I tell you straight, Boss," or, to me, "I tell you straight, Boss Lady." He played his lackey role to the hilt, aware that we knew it was a game to him. When we asked him how much we owed him for a day's work, he would flash a disarming grin and say, "Whatever's fair to you, Boss." (The drivers generally get more money that way than if they just charged a flat rate. It's cheap anyhow—a car and driver for the whole day and night for about $12, split four ways between the Schmidts and us.)

The ride out to Blance's each morning was always interesting, this Sunday no exception. When we'd exhausted Boykho with questions about the Philippines, he turned the tables on us, wanting to know all about home. His impression of Chicago was typical of foreigners—all he knew about was violent crime and gangsters. He even gave us some insight into mob influence in the Philippines, hinting at a Philippine connection to the solving of the Richard Speck case, in which eight nurses including some Filipinos were murdered in Chicago a few years ago.

We knew our way around pretty well by now, having been in Manila about a week. Boykho didn't have to ask directions to the Healers anymore, and neither did we when we rode with another driver. We waved to the same schoolchildren every day as they walked past Blance's house. And we felt freer to talk with other patients who were waiting to see him. Most were natives, for whom Boykho would translate our comments and questions, but we did run into some Americans and some Germans.

This day, there was an elderly Filipino couple. Ironically, their son and daughter-in-law are both M.D.'s practicing in Chicago! So what were they doing at the Healer's? Blance, they told us, had cured the woman of cancer, which had been medically diagnosed and the cure confirmed. We asked what their kids thought of their coming to see the Healers. The woman replied, "Oh, we just do not talk to them about it. They would not understand." We laughed, knowing exactly what she meant. The Philippine Medical Association, reportedly taking its cues from the A.M.A., discourages Filipino doctors from taking the Healers seriously or even investigating their work. (Unlike the U.S. government, which seems to be in active collusion with the A.M.A. to suppress information about the Healers, the Philippine government has requested the P.M.A. to leave the Healers alone.)

Blance wanted to get rid of the largest lump in

Don's neck. Don was very relieved, because that was one thing he'd been discouraged about a few days before. First, Blance shaved the back of Don's neck with a razor blade so the hair would not get in the way. Then he used my finger to make an opening about ¾ of an inch long. He pressed down the edges of the opening with the fingers of one hand, and used the other to reach for the material near the surface, removing some tiny clumps of whitish substance. Finally, he pulled out a sizeable mass and some surrounding loose gooey tissue, showing the material to Don. (Because of its light color and shape, Don described it as looking like a little brain, which of course gave rise to a still continuing series of jokes!) It must have been imbedded fairly far down in his neck, because when I went over to take pictures of the opening, I could see blood pulsing through the artery a good ½ inch below the surface. Yet there was no bleeding. Blance put a bandaid over the hole and said it would close up in a couple of days. I could see, and Don could feel, an actual indentation in his neck just to the right of the opening, the spot where the lump had previously been. Blance remarked that the growth, deposit or whatever it was could have become cancerous if he hadn't taken it out.

Boykho was in rare form on the way back to the hotel. We passed by some billboards advertising martial arts films (some of which came to the States under new titles in the martial arts craze that began here a few months later). Don had been into both karate and aikido, so he and Boykho were discussing the disciplines. Boykho said his favorite defense form was Torun. We'd never heard of that one, and said so. By now, Boykho was laughing. "You know, when guy comes after you, you pick up your feet—to run!"

Atrocious pun, but we went into hysterics over it, and Boykho couldn't figure out why. But it seems he was serious, that it was not an intentional pun—it was just his accent!

ALEX II

Our appointment with Alex was at 9 a.m. Chuck Isaacs arrived at 10 minutes after nine and said Alex would be up to the room in a few minutes. When he got there about 10 minutes later, he told us he needed some things to work with—he had brought nothing at all with him. Boykho and I ran to a drugstore a couple of blocks from the hotel and bought a small bottle of Johnson & Johnson Baby Oil, some cotton, and a bottle of rubbing alcohol. We stopped at the hotel desk and asked for some notebook paper for Alex to use for his x-rays; they gave us hotel letterhead, which I cut into quarters.

Between 9:45 and 10:30, we watched Alex as he worked on each of us in turn, fast and furiously; we could hardly believe what he accomplished in that short time. And it could not have been faked, for not only did we provide the equipment, but Alex was wearing cuffless, pocketless, skintight slacks and a short-sleeved, transparent barong-tagalog shirt. (Besides, we have had some experience with sleight-of-hand magic through Don's son Tony, who is a magician, and knew pretty well what to watch for.)

We wanted to make sure we got good films of Alex because, for one thing, he was an excellent Healer who deserved to become better known, and for another, his attitude was beautiful. He was not a publicity hound but was more than willing to cooperate with us to get sufficient light for our pictures. We stripped one of the beds in our room down to stark white sheet and moved it directly under the window. We took down the curtains and the blinds to let in as much sun as possible, took the shades off all the lamps and fixtures, and turned on all the lights. We had not brought along auxiliary bulbs of any kind, figuring that the available light camera with high speed film would suffice, but for the most part, the films came out on the dark side and had to be lightened in processing except for this session with Alex.

Alex worked on Don first. In less than two minutes (I know the time because it was a half a reel of film) he had made openings and closed three separate spots along Don's spine, removing blood clots and calcium deposits. He began just under the right shoulder blade. He wriggled his fingers and out popped some unhealthy tissue, which he placed in a tray of water (we didn't even have a dish, so we had to use the tray our water pitcher was on). Don said the back rub felt good. Back rub indeed—Alex's hand slid over to the left side of the spine and took some more goop out. Don couldn't even tell there was more than massage taking place. About 20 seconds after he had started on the first place, the second one was already closed! He moved his hand down the spine and made an opening near the small of Don's back, and again brought out some blood clots on the ends of his fingers, then it was over. Alex had performed three operations in a row, almost effortlessly, in one smooth motion.

Don, who was very comfortable, flipped over on his back, so Alex could work on his heart. Years before, Don had been medically diagnosed as having a leaky heart valve. It wasn't too serious except that it did cause him some pain in cold weather, and sometimes shortness of breath. For two years he had resorted to nitroglycerin on occasion, although for the past ten years or so, just vitamin E seemed to control it well except in cold weather, or after a couple of drinks. The combination of the excitement, pace and air conditioning must have set it off, because Don had chest pains the night before. He mentioned the pains to Alex but gave him no further information; the Healer tuned in psychically to diagnose the problem and shortly announced that there was a blood clot near the valve leading into one chamber of the heart. Alex hadn't even touched Don, had no background on his case, yet his conclusion seemed to coincide with the medical one! Being a believer in "preventive maintenance" (his term), Alex declared he would "fix it" to avert a potential heart attack.

First, he rubbed some baby oil on Don's chest, and put a piece of our paper over it. He prayed for a few seconds before lifting the paper off and holding it up to the camera. We could see a clear, light spot in the middle of the oil stain which Alex said pinpointed the difficulty. It was a simple operation, done with no fanfare: Alex merely twisted his right hand over the area of the spot on Don's chest that had shown on the x-ray, and poked his fingers through the skin; there was a little trickle of blood that ran down Don's side onto the bed. When Alex brought his hand out a few seconds later, there was a large clump of bloody material sitting in the cup of his fingers. He gave it to me and asked me to throw it out. It felt gooey and rubbery, like coagulating blood, but it didn't occur to us to keep it for analysis. That was that—it was over literally before Don realized what was happening, and he has not had any trouble with his heart since then. Following the operation, Chuck, who had been assisting Alex, did a spiritual healing on Don's heart, too, putting his hand on Don's chest, covering his face with his other hand, and meditating. He stayed in that position for a couple of minutes, explaining that he was sending Don energy to help the heart rebalance and regenerate itself.

Don sat up so Alex could look at his ears and try to get rid of that infernal ringing. Alex picked up a wad of dry cotton—I know it was dry because I handed it to him out of the package Boykho and I had bought earlier—and put it up against Don's ear. He tilted Don's head to that side. A few seconds later, he brought away the cotton, dripping wet, and wrung it out into the tray. He repeated this three or four more times, bringing water out of Don's ear. Don said he felt something happening, felt as though a wall were being lifted inside his head. There was less pressure, and the roaring seemed to lessen. Up to his ear went his watch, but he still could not hear it tick, and even though he said he could hear external noises more clearly, as though a baffle had been removed, the ringing was still there. Alex said there was water trapped behind the eardrums. But he couldn't do too much on any one person at one time, and unfortunately, the opportunity never arose for him to do Don's other ear, much to Don's disappointment.

Chuck continued to work alongside Alex, picking up things on his own as well as explaining to us what Alex was doing. He was trying to be helpful both to us and to Alex, but the truth was, he wasn't really needed all that much. He was a little patronizing towards us; no matter how much we told him, he could not accept that we already had some understanding of the whole thing. We realized that Chuck, much as we liked him, was letting his ego get in the way. So who doesn't once in a while? (Including me, whose first chance to be an honest-to-God author was and is quite an ego trip!)

Boykho was in the room with us, too. He was coming in handy for translation when Alex's meager English failed him, especially on more technical words. He had wanted very much to watch Alex work again and was getting really interested in the whole healing thing. But as fascinated as he was, he refused Alex's offer of a checkup.

I asked Alex to look me over and do whatever he deemed necessary. Right away, he mentioned a problem with my ovaries. He told me there were blood clots that had to come out, so I lay face up on the bed. I was wearing hiphugger jeans, so I didn't have to get undressed or anything. Alex began to push his hands against my stomach. I tensed up. He ordered me to relax and not worry, thinking that I was nervous, when I just happened to be very ticklish there! Then after he began to massage the stomach again, I felt a pinching. "Am I open?" I inquired. Don and Alex laughed. "Open?" Alex exclaimed, "I close it already." He showed me the bloody material he had removed. I didn't even know when the operation began and ended; the pinching must have been at the instant he jerked his hand back out. He did a quick magnetic healing on my eyes by pressing his hands against my eyes and forehead. He said he wanted to take out some blockage from behind each ear—apparently some that Virgilio and Blance had missed—but that would have to wait until the next

time we came to his place. We were again impressed
with the consistency of the various Healers' analyses
of the same case, as with my eyes and Don's ears.

We called Don's folks and the Mortons when we
were pretty sure Alex was through with us for the
day. While we were waiting for them to get to our
room, Alex spotted a copy of Tony's book on our
dresser. He pointed to the portrait of Tony on the
flyleaf, "Very rich. Very famous." He didn't seem upset to discover we had been seeing Tony, but we felt
he didn't quite approve of Tony, either. I told Alex I
was going to write a book and he would be in it. Grinning slyly, he asked if we would make him as famous
as Tony, and Don said we hoped so. Alex, then, was
not entirely egoless, but at least he wasn't obnoxious
about it. He consented to do a taped interview with
us when he was through working on the other members of our group.

Dad had recurrent pains in his back, which Alex
said were caused by water in the lungs. He picked up
an enormous ball of cotton and asked Dad to take off
his shirt and sit on the bed. He held the cotton
against Dad's back; it became quickly drenched and
water ran down onto the mattress. Alex tossed out
the cotton and placed a fresh wad against Dad's back
(about ⅓ of the way down and slightly to the left of
his spine). It was sopping wet in a few seconds. Alex
took more cotton and did it again, wringing the excess water into the dish. There must have been at
least a cup of water by the time he was through. The
Healer told Dad to take a deep breath—impossible
for him to do before, without pain. Now there was no
pain at all. Alex hadn't even made an opening; the
water just came up through the skin. (We found out
when Dad passed away late in 1975 that his kidneys

had been failing for years due to his heart medication; thus the water might be explained.)

Alex did some of his "preventive maintenance" on Marge Morton, who had a clot near her heart which Alex said could eventually cause a stroke. Marge went into the bathroom to take off her sweater, and returned with a towel tied precariously around her midriff, somewhat embarrassed. It shouldn't have bothered her—we were all one big family by that time (despite the spats) and besides, she could have asked us to step out while Alex worked on her, like I had done at Virgilio's. She lay on the bed, face up. Alex drew the sheet up over her and working near the edge of the towel, reached in under the towel to withdraw the clot, which was about the size of a dime. The operation took only a half a minute and preserved her modesty.

Nate was next. Alex did a couple of things for him: one, he reached into his back just above the kidneys and unpinched some nerves, and two, he cleaned out some deposits from around the heart. He also worked on Nate's stomach or thereabouts, after Nate asked him to relieve the pain of an ulcer. We couldn't really see what he was doing, although he did take out some kind of icky looking tissue. Alex didn't know what it was; he just knew it didn't belong there.

Don's mother didn't want to have anything done. She was afraid, and/or was convinced (still is, even though the Healers probably gave Dad a couple of extra years) that the whole thing was a fake, because of some alleged chicanery she supposedly witnessed but never reported directly to us. Don took the opportunity to ask Alex to look at his thumb, the tendons of which had been severed in an accident, causing him to lose control of his right hand every so often. It could be embarrassing, all of a sudden dropping a drink for no visible reason, but Alex couldn't help him; as is often the case with the Healers, he was reluctant to work where there was scar tissue from conventional surgery.

Jack and Mary Ann were waiting for us in Joe Bush's room. They were late because an acquaintance of theirs had arrived in Manila that morning to see the Healers—a paraplegic woman named Pat—and we had suggested that they take her to see Mrs. D. (They came back unimpressed with Mrs. D. but Joe thought he might try to get out there later in the afternoon.) Pat had gone back to her own hotel to rest.

Alex did magnetic healings on Joe's spine and head, and took out some more blood clots, essentially the same things that Tony and Virgilio had done for him. Joe realized by now that his recovery would probably take a long time, but he was patient. Right in the middle of working on Joe, Alex looked up at Don and said, matter-of-factly, as if he were talking about the weather, "You have the Power to heal. I will help you." I was reminded of the comment Virgilio's assistant had made to Marge Morton, that two in our group had the Gift. Well, there was one! Don was not surprised; after all, we had been practicing spiritual and magnetic healing back home for a year or so with some success. He merely nodded, although we both felt Alex was referring to material healing, too. Alex promised to talk with Don later to transfer some ability that would help him develop the Gift. (No, Don does not do material healing. Yes, he would like to go to the Philippines to study with Alex and learn it some day.)

While we set up the tape recorder, Alex told us about a 17-year-old boy whom he had cured of a fatal kidney disease. The boy was the son of the Chief-of-Staff of a large hospital in Manila. When the doctors gave up, his father sent for Alex as a last resort, having heard of him through another doctor who went to Alex for heart treatment and occasionally sent patients to him on the q.t. So the father snuck Alex into his son's room and stood guard outside while Alex worked. The boy recovered fully; now that doctor refers people to the Healers, too. Officially, for the medical records, the boy had a "spontaneous remission" of the fatal illness, a phrase about as meaningful as "coincidence." (We ran into another doctor at Alex's one day. He told me that he's under heart treatment from the Healer and frequently brings his own patients to see him. Such cases of M.D.'s working "underground" with Healers isn't that uncommon, though they don't talk about it much.)

Alex agreed to the taped interview on one condition—that he be allowed to speak in Tagalog, with Boykho translating. That was fine with us. But a funny thing happened: once Alex started talking, he used English and only rarely needed Boykho's help. And Boykho actually began anticipating Alex's answers to our questions, a couple of times answering for him. The interview was beautiful, much longer than we had planned. We said thank you and nearly ended it several times, then Alex would begin a new thought or someone would think of another question. We have at least a half-hour of candid conversation with Alex, about his life, his work, what he does for certain types of cases, how he keeps his power, etc. Alex said that when he was a small child in a miserable lowland village, he prayed to be able to do something for his people, who were very poor. He didn't specify that he wanted to be a Healer, just that he wanted to help. So every day while his little friends were playing after school, he would go home and pray and read the Bible. That went on for about six years, till he was 13; at that time, he had a dream that he could heal people, but he didn't really believe. Still, he started practicing magnetic healings and when he was 17, the healings became effective. He kept working and meditating and just a few years ago received the ability to do the material healing. It just happened one day while he was doing a massage: the person opened up and he did psychic surgery. To keep this Gift, Alex has to meditate every night and read Scripture. He likes to do his meditation between midnight and 1 a.m. because "it is quiet and the channels are open." That's also when he sends out his absent healing. Alex feels he would lose his power if he asked for money. (He does accept donations, gratefully, but he never asks.) He did say he was glad when the Espiritista changed its policy of not allowing the Healers to accept anything at all for their work. He says it is okay to be paid as long as the Healers do not use their Gift to get rich, or begin to take their ability for granted. That made sense to us, because otherwise, the patients would be getting something for nothing—probably not good for their own spiritual development.

Alex described case after case that he had worked on: cancers, improvement in mentally retarded children, and on and on. I asked him about helping people whose problems are not physical, but are in their heads. My wording confused him; he didn't understand the question, so Boykho rephrased it in Tagalog. Alex nodded: yes, he can help emotionally disturbed people, if they are ready for it. He doesn't just cure them instantly, though—he helps them see what is really wrong, helps them open up in their hearts, and gives them the energy and willingness to help themselves. But they have to have that spiritual awakening to make real progress. Psychiatrists tend to agree that they can't help someone who doesn't really want it or who won't work on their problems themselves.

We wanted to get him to talk about karma, without using the word ourselves, so we asked if there's ever a time when he can not help a person because God feels that person should keep the ailment. At first, he didn't quite understand what we were leading up to. We asked the question three or four times in different ways. Finally, Joe, who had not caught on to our trying to get Alex to introduce the word "karma" into the conversation, asked if there is ever a karmic reason for a person to be sick. Alex said yes, of course, but he could even help karmic afflictions if the person is ready to be helped, ready to dump his karma, in effect, and if it is his own karma to do so.

Don asked if a patient has to have faith to get help from Alex. The Healer smiled, "No. I have enough faith for both." It does help, naturally, for the patient to have some faith, but it is not essential. How about the openings? Alex explained that he wouldn't have to do as many as he does, but that sometimes the patient accepts the healing better if there is an opening, in other words, it is a psychological boost. As to his actual technique, Don asked Alex how come he does not leave a scar. Alex grinned, "You want scar? I give you if you want."

Some of the Healers claim to have only one or two Spirit Guides. Alex says he becomes a medium for many different entities when he heals. On days when his Power is at its utmost, he said, it is usually a saint working through him. The saints can come through when a Healer's vibration is at a really high level, or when they pray hard enough for extra power on a particularly rough day or case. We have heard of Matthew, Mark and Mary Magdalene, for example, coming through various Healers; Alex told us that when Mark makes contact with him, there is nothing he can't do.

We hardly knew where the time had gone, all of us were so enthralled with Alex. We'd been talking almost an hour. There was a fast friendship developing among Boykho, Don and Alex which everyone was aware of—it had to be karmic. Boykho said we should start a business of sending people to see Alex, that he could drive them there. We do give their names—along with names of other Healers and helpful contacts—to people who are serious about going to the Philippines, although Boykho is no longer a tourist guide. But it is not a business arrangement, just a personal one, and we never give the information to people who don't specifically ask for it or whom we don't have a positive feeling about.

ESPIRITISTA SERVICE AT VIRGILIO'S

Boykho picked up the Schmidts and Don and me, then we all went to the Aurelio Hotel to get the Schmidts' friend Pat. I was surprised when we met her because I had been picturing a chunky, middle-aged woman. Pat was 22, slim, delicate, almost childlike; and shy, but certainly brave, having traveled all the way to the Philippines by herself to see what help she might get in walking again. She couldn't even get out of her seat for the whole 18 hour flight. Boykho loaded her folding wheelchair into the trunk, after he and Don assisted her in sliding off it into the front seat of the car. Jack and Mary Ann rode with them, Don and Joe Bush and I piled into a cab behind them, and Don's folks and the Mortons followed in another cab, all heading to Virgilio's. I was most anxious to talk with Virgilio again, as I'd had two dreams about him since Tuesday (five days ago)—both concerning a past life together.

Sister Rose met us at the doorway and asked us to wait in the living room. She was afraid that bringing Pat and her chair in would disrupt the worship service, which had just begun. Also, it was very hot and crowded in the main waiting room where the services were held, so we'd be more comfortable in the family living quarters. (Pat, in addition to being paralyzed from the waist down, could not perspire, making the heat especially hard on her.) Somebody, Rose I suppose, came up with a couple of bottles of chilled Orange Crush, which were passed around among our whole group.

A striped cotton curtain divided the living quarters of the house from the makeshift chapel; it was clean but worn, about ten feet wide, hanging from ceiling to floor. I crept up to the curtain, cautiously drew back an edge and peeped around to watch a trance medium giving messages in Tagalog to various people in the congregation from souls on "the other side" of death. It looked like any spiritualist service we'd been to in the States, and the crowd was very psychically aware. I'd only been there a few seconds when people started turning to stare at me. I couldn't move the curtain the slightest bit without being detected. Rose asked me to rejoin the others in the front room. She said my "strong presence was upsetting the vibrations." Don was watching from the opposite corner of the drapery but she let him stay—apparently his emanations were under better control than mine.

While the service was going on, Virgilio wandered in to say hello to us. I told him about the recurring dream: he and I had been cousins, but I couldn't place where or when. Virgilio didn't show any particular interest; as a matter of fact, he laughed, even though he knew I was serious. Disappointed, I dropped the subject (again) while Don made arrangements for him to come work on us at the hotel the next day. Then I chatted with Sister Rose for a long time. She said she had known me before, which is probably true, although I haven't gotten any data on it, and she told me all about herself (the story we'd

heard from other sources about her being a pharmacist, etc.) and gave me a typewritten sheet to make
copies of—her story, including her conversion to
spiritualism and coming to work in Virgilio's minis-
try, along with some Franciscan prayers and other
information on healing, all in broken English. She
also mentioned something about working at a home
for unwed mothers in her spare time, and said she'd
appreciate a donation for that if we could afford it.
And she asked if I could do her a favor—please send
her a couple bottles of Clairol hair color, which she
couldn't find in the Philippines. Rose and I sat on the
couch and talked like that for about a half hour, until
she left to get "a token" she had for me. It was a
lovely little shoulder bag made all of seashells. She
wrote later and said she had taken gifts for the rest
of our group to the airport at our scheduled departure time, but wasn't able to find us.

The service had begun at about 3:30, about a half
hour before we arrived. But it was 5:30 before
Virgilio started working. We again were asked to observe from the enclosed porch off his operating room.
I watched for only a short time, then had to leave,
because I found myself staring at Virgilio, and every
time I did, he'd turn around and give me a sharp look,
not nasty but disconcerted. Something was certainly
running between us, and I didn't want to disturb him
while he was trying to heal people. So I went out of
sight, to a place in the hall to the kitchen where I
could watch but not be seen. Romeo and Mom were
talking up a storm behind me. She paid him 10 pesos
for a large bottle of homemade, "blessed" coconut oil,
which he told her to rub on anytime there was pain
from headache, upset stomach, etc. (Blessed meaning
Virgilio had prayed over it.) We still have almost all

our oil—we either forget to use it, or are afraid to waste it on everyday ills.

At last, it was time for Virgilio to work on us. He did a magnetic healing on my eyes; while he was doing it, I went into a deep trance, during which I saw the same scene from that darned dream, in more detail. I vaguely felt Virgilio tap my forehead to indicate he was finished, but I didn't want to come out of it. He tapped me again. I knew I had to get up because the others were waiting. But it had been so comfortable, and above all, I needed to find out more about what and who I was seeing.

Virgilio proceeded to work on the others. He and Don lifted Pat out of her wheelchair and onto the table, then he removed some blood clots from her spine and legs. She seemed disappointed that she felt no immediate difference, but Joe Bush tried to encourage her. There was an instant empathy between them, since their problems were outwardly similar. Joe felt that he was getting help, slowly but surely; he said he would stay as long as it took, which he realized might be several more weeks.

When Virgilio took a cigarette break, I stopped him in the hall. I wanted to ask him if I could invite Rose (the girl we'd met at Mrs. D.'s) to see him work at our hotel the next day, as she had never seen psychic surgery. He said it was okay. As he started to walk away from me, he suddenly wheeled around and grabbed my arm. The air between us was almost electric. He appeared startled, as if he had not consciously turned back to me. He told me I would be returning to the Philippines again "one day." I said, "I was right, wasn't I?" Virgilio nodded and asked me to tell him about the dream. There were two children in the dream, a boy about 10 or 11 and a girl a couple of years younger. They were riding in a reed boat on a large lake and had to race to shore to beat a storm that was brewing up in the middle of the lake. The boat overturned close to shore and they had to swim the rest of the way in. They were dressed identically, in short white tunics. That was all I had for the time being. (As I got more details later, I told or wrote them to Virgilio.)

Virgilio and I just stood there staring at each other. It was so strange: neither of us could move, as if we were riveted to the floor in one position. Sister Rose walked by us and did a classic double-take, breaking the spell. She was picking up the strength of the vibration between us. She took my hand and declared, "You have the Power." Virgilio nodded and went back to his workroom. I now knew how Don had felt when he'd heard it from Alex; I was close to tears. Sister Rose led me over to the sofa and sat me down next to Mary Ann. She directed Mary Ann to lean on me whenever things got rough or discouraging. Mary Ann replied, "I know. I already have."

Virgilio, meantime, was working on Don's dad, treating his diabetes. Dad was face-up on the table, with his shirt pulled up over his chest. Virgilio inspected the abdomen then picked up a spoon and pressed it against the skin. In a few seconds, the spoon was filled with blood, which he dumped in a pan. There was no opening per se, but Virgilio took out several tablespoons of blood. It was the only time Dad had mentioned the blood sugar problem to a Healer and the only time anybody worked on it. But the results bear it out—Dad had a test when he came back and it was normal for the first time in years. He continued to take his medication, but only half as much, to make sure the diabetes didn't recur.

We and the Schmidts were invited to Boykho's brother's home for dinner that night, so we had to leave long before Virgilio was finished for the day. We left Virgilio's place in Quezon City, dropped Pat off at her hotel (next door to ours), changed clothes, then went back to Quezon, all in about an hour. We were ready to relax.

Boykho's older brother is in the import-export business—French perfumes and other such luxury goods—and must do well. The house is in a well-to-do area and is completely surrounded by a high concrete wall. Boykho pulled into the driveway and honked, and his sister-in-law came out and opened the gate to let us drive in. I'd already met Mr. and Mrs. Kho, and she ran out and threw her arms around me. Boykho introduced other brothers and sisters and nieces and nephews and we never did get everybody straight. Such a beautiful, closeknit family! With their warm, sincere welcome, we felt right at home. The men and Mary Ann and I sat on the patio and had a beer while the other women got supper ready; they wouldn't hear of our lending a hand. There were little lizards all over the house and garage keeping insects away.

We ate supper inside in shifts, and what a feast! Mrs. Kho and a couple of the older girls served us chicken, shrimp, pork, rice, three salads, chinese vegetables, beer, coffee, fresh fruits, and cake. We ate till we thought we'd burst. It was so nice to be in a home atmosphere instead of the hotel; as good as a big hotel can be, it just can't be that personal and cozy.

Right in the middle of dinner, I heard someone say, "Peru." The someone, I discovered to my surprise, was me. It had just hit me in a flash where that dream was set, and I'd said it aloud. Throughout the evening and off and on for several months, I would see those scenes, ever in more detail. In fact, each time I rewrote this section of the book, I would get more information. The two children often took that boat out for a picnic and swim. It leaked, and they had to patch it over and over. They were not supposed to use it at all (they'd found it washed up on the beach one time after a rainstorm) but kids are kids! They used to sit on the beach—a sort of special place for them—and talk for hours. The boy was Virgilio and the girl, me, and we were cousins. The two children were very close and made a pledge to each other to always stay together and depend on each other. One day, they returned to their homes, in a village of stone houses that looked very Incan, and felt something was wrong. My father told me that my uncle—Virgilio's father—was dead. He was some kind of priest or medicine man, and now his son would have to take his place. I was very sad, for I knew it meant a long separation. The two children stood hand in hand at the funeral, dressed in long white mourning tunics, crying, but it wasn't, as the adults thought, entirely because of the death; the next day, the boy would be taken away. He must have been 12 or 13 at the time. He was away for more than four years, then there was a big welcoming procession and ceremony for his return. I stood in the crowd waiting for him to spot me, as he was carried by on a litter, looking very grown up and regal. But he looked right at me and didn't recognize me, even though I was waving at him with a secret childhood signal. I was really upset and tried to run up to the litter, but my parents held me back because it was forbidden. Then he spotted me. He could not come to me, ever again, however, for he was sacred or something. And I was supposed to marry someone else. (I do not know if I did.) I did see him frequently, because I became a kind of maid-in-waiting to the priestesses in the temple where he healed people. We never spoke and I missed him terribly; he was always near but it was frustratingly impossible to be close as adults.

So no wonder there was such a strong, karmic vibe between Virgilio and me—a deep friendship, nipped at its height, had carried over. And no wonder he's such a fine Healer now, not being the first time. Virgilio never told me his interpretation of it all. I do know it would be difficult for me to work with him if Don and I return to the Philippines to learn healing, so the karma will have to be worked through at another place and time or level.

THE SECOND WEEK BEGINS

Our second Monday in the Philippines, the start of the second week: we could hardly believe that half of our long-planned vacation was over; but we were so at home there, and had experienced so much, it seemed we'd been there longer, so it was equally strange to think half of it was yet to come. It would start with another heavily scheduled, long day. Boykho was to take us to Blance's, then to Makati to pick up my friend Rose, Virgilio would be at the hotel early in the afternoon, and later we were to go to Mrs. D.'s for the Novena.

There was a communication gap with Boykho. He failed to pick us up, so we took a cab to Blance's and asked the driver to wait for us. I asked Blance if he could remove several moles that bothered me occasionally—one under a breast where my bra hit it all the time, two on my back, also on the bra line, one on my right arm that kept catching on long-sleeved sweaters, and one on my hip, just under the band of my hip hugger jeans. I pointed this out so Blance would know it wasn't just vanity that prompted me, because the Healers don't usually do cosmetic surgery per se. Typical of Blance, the procedure was a combination of spirit healing and folk medicine. He brushed each mole with alcohol first. Then, one at a time, he struck a match and lit each one. It hurt like hell. I took deep breaths and dug my hands into Don's arm so hard it almost broke the skin. But it was over fast, and there was one odd thing about the way those moles were burned out—not a single hair in or around them was singed at all, just the moles themselves! They did blister, so Blance gently placed bandaids on them. A couple of the moles have started to grow back. But on the rest there is hardly any scarring, and that's a blessing for me, because I've had moles removed by doctors before and every one of them formed a big, rough, ugly keloid.

We found Rose's home with no trouble. Don waited in the car while I went in to get her. Her mother was expecting us, and gave me an embroidered doily as a keepsake. Rose, knowing I was sensitive to the tropical sun, gave me a native straw hat. Don, Rose and I went back to the hotel for breakfast, but for some reason, Rose was afraid of Don and uneasy about talking in front of him. So he left to get some more film while we continued the conversation.

Rose couldn't get over the fact that we'd been married for 2½ years and had no babies, saying the same things as the Healers, like "a pity," (and also "such a shame" that Don is "too short" for me!) For Rose, as for most Philippine women, the idea of women's lib, women having a career, or being childless by choice even temporarily was literally and figuratively foreign. She kept looking at the door, positive that Don would come storming in, very mad at me for being away from him so long. She could not understand a man who was not jealous of every minute of his wife's time or who trusted his wife alone. All Rose could talk about was getting to the States. It was like those stories of immigrants who thought the streets would be paved with gold or something. Filipinos living in the U.S. must tell their friends back home only the good things! Rose was even considering marrying a G-I whom she didn't care for too much, just to get to the U.S. That was as unthinkable to me as my situation was to her. So I quickly changed the subject—I started telling her all about Virgilio (subconsciously matchmaking, no doubt). What I didn't count on was that Rose was something of a social snob, and the Healers have no place in that middle-class status game of the urban Filipinos. Besides, Rose was becoming so attached to me that she actually appeared jealous of any attention I paid to other people.

Virgilio arrived after lunch, bringing two of the women of his entourage; his landlady, Mrs. Mendoza, was one, but the other one we did not know. Don and I had been privately referring to his assistants as his "groupies" which was not far from the truth. (Except for Sister Rose who was a psychic in her own right.) The vibration between Virgilio and me was as strong as ever. He walked in, squeezed my hand, and winked, "Hi, Cousin." Immediately I felt myself going into trance, so I sat crosslegged in a corner and focused on the scene with the children, while Virgilio worked on the others. Every time I would open my eyes, he would sense it and turn and stare at me. He was not working up to par, and therefore was doing mostly magnetic healings. He took a look at Rose's "evil" eye and found nothing. And he ran his hands over my eyes but was so distracted that I felt nothing aside from the karmic thing.

I thought maybe I was the cause of the problem, so I decided not to go with the others to see Pat at the Aurelio next door. I waited outside her room with the cassette recorder, hoping to catch Virgilio for an interview when he was through. After 10 minutes or so, Don came out to get me. Virgilio asked what happened to me, again addressing me as "cousin." But he knew the answer and he knew why I had not gone in. Virgilio told Pat he could have her on her feet in two to three weeks if he could work on her every day, and knowing that she didn't have a lot of money, Mrs. Mendoza offered to put her up in the guest room at her house. Pat was delighted. We had mixed feelings about the arrangement—it might make it awkward for her to get out to see other Healers. We voiced our opinion out of Virgilio's earshot, but it had to be her decision; we wouldn't even be in town after today.

Virgilio took his leave. Rose and I went for a walk and said goodbye for the time being. We would see her later at Mrs. D.'s, and she also wanted to meet us at Alex's the next morning before we left for Baguio. Don and I barely had time to eat, get showered and changed, and get to Makati on time. It seemed as if we were always rushing somewhere, even when we should have had hours to spare!

MRS. D. II

Novena means renewal of faith, and this particular Novena eve was the ceremonial start of the Easter season. Again, we had trouble finding Mrs. D.'s house, so we were a half hour late. Dinah and the ex-cripple teenaged boy were waiting to drive us to the religious service, which was already underway on the roof of the apartment building where we had seen the crucifix the other day. We walked up four flights of rickety, narrow steps to reach the roof. The crucifix had been set up on a makeshift altar, the whole structure draped in sampaguita, its aroma filling the night air. About 60 people stood in a semicircle around the altar, many of whom had been at Mrs. D.'s Saturday; some nodded in recognition. An old woman was reading a liturgy in Tagalog. She then led the people in singing, and their voices were strong and clear, full of meaning, the melodies and language haunting and powerful.

I looked out over the city from the edge of the roof. The sight was breathtaking. The sky was midnight blue, with stars glittering like crystal overhead. We could see the lights of Hotel Row and the harbor, and the far-off glow from the islands of Bataan and Corregidor. I rejoined the worship circle, my eyes brimming with tears, praying to myself, half listening to Dinah as she translated the Bible verses the old woman was reading. Rose slipped in beside me and handed me a book—a Tagalog/English-English/Tagalog dictionary. She made me promise to try to learn Tagalog before we returned to the Philippines again (a promise I haven't been able to keep, unable to find anyone to teach me). I quickly looked up how to say "thank you" and whispered, "Salamat." She grinned. Virgilio had told me I would be coming back, and I prayed he was right.

Something was happening inside these people. Their faith was open and pure. The service itself was pretty much a standard mass with group responses, etc., but it was different than any I had been to in Mexico or even at Notre Dame in Paris. For the first time, I had an insight into how the Catholic church can have such a hold on a poor nation's populace. Although these folks were middle class, their religion was the only real thing in their lives. It was more than ritual—it was deep and heartfelt, with no trappings. This must have been what early Christianity was like, before politics and ego trips took over. There was no priest here, no building fund drive, no power plays. It was a group of sincere, humble people, unabashedly giving themselves to God and each other. And to me, it was a sort of revelation.

After the service, all the people filed towards the stairs, still singing hymns and chanting prayers. Dinah had us in tow. On the way down, somebody handed us little packets of candy and some candles. We ducked out through the low doorway and, finding ourselves surrounded by begging children, joyously followed the example of the others, and handed out the candy, part of the Novena tradition. One of the men lit our candles, asking if we had Novenas in the

States; not exactly like this, I explained, although some of the ethnic communities have similar ceremonies and activities.

Someone brought the crucifix downstairs, and everyone lined up to kiss the Christ's feet. We did, too, of course, being so moved by the whole thing so far that we wouldn't have thought of scoffing. Then Don was accorded a great honor—he, a foreigner and a non-Catholic, was asked to be the first to carry the cross in the procession. We were really touched. One of the men from Mrs. D.'s showed him how to hold it, and ordered everyone to line up behind him. He steered Don in the right direction, and Don began to walk out of the alley into the street. The parade wound its way through the side streets of the parish, the people singing the Tagalog version of "The Lord's Prayer" all the while, and taking lights from each other's candles whenever they'd blow out. There was some laughing and talking, and children playing tag among the marchers. Nevertheless, the vibration was very high, like a moving mantra, flowing its way through the village, its energy moving from person to person in giant patterns. It was total communication, like what happened in the Biblical descriptions of the Holy Spirit moving among the people.

After a few blocks, they asked me to take my turn leading the procession. I'm not as strong as I might appear, and that cross was very heavy. I prayed I would be able to hold onto it, and suddenly it seemed to lift upward, to feel lighter. I stumbled along through brick paths and ditches. Mr. D. marched alongside, gently steering me over rocks and whispering directions, once in a while correcting the position of the cross so it would be straight upright. It was unusally hot and humid, plus the fragrance of the bouquets of sampaguita on the crucifix was almost overpowering; I was getting dizzy, but was determined not to falter. Eventually, Mr. D. asked if it would be alright for another person to take over. Only a few of the people would be afforded the honor of carrying the cross, and many were clamoring around me. The boy who until a few weeks ago had not even been able to walk gingerly and reverently took it out of my hands. I took his candle and fell in behind. Don was lost somewhere back in the crowd.

The candle was a cheap one and the rapidly melting tallow was dripping all over my hands. (I didn't pay much attention to it at the time, but the next day I noticed my jeans and sandals were covered with yellow wax.) The cobblestones were hard under my feet, but since most of the natives were wearing no shoes at all as a symbol of humility, obedience, and repentance, I felt selfish and unsacrificing in comparison. Just then, Dinah ran up and handed me a glass of ice water, and wiped my streaming forehead with her handkerchief. The cross-bearer turned at a house; we followed him up the outside steps, to a second story apartment.

It was a simple building, really little more than a two story hut, with a floor of unfinished wood. There was a breeze blowing through the cutout that served as a picture window. Turning my face to catch it, I happened to glance out, and was tremendously moved by the sight below. I had been in the front of the procession so I hadn't paid any attention to anything but keeping my balance and seeing through the darkness. It seems that as we passed people's homes, they came out and joined the line, all carrying candles. Now there was a stream of hundreds of shadowy, candle-lit figures down in the street, stretching for several blocks into the Philippine night. That did it: I began to cry unashamedly. Don more or less materialized beside me, handing me a drink of water; I shook my head and pointed out the window. And he, too, became choked up. There was a brief ceremony in the apartment, during which we all knelt as the owner placed a statue of the Virgin Mary on his mantle. There were only a dozen or so of us inside; the rest continued singing outside until we made our way back down the steps. When the parade started again, it was Mrs. D. who took up the cross, the first time we had seen her that evening. She walked with remarkable strength and dignity for a woman so tiny, frail and weak, but she couldn't manage it for very long, so her husband drove her home. Nevertheless, the people knew their "Tita Ester" had been there, and were uplifted.

The next stop on the route was a larger, nicer home. We had fallen back into the middle of the parade, but the people parted silently to let us through into the house to hear the old woman who had conducted the Novena service lead a choral reading. Several dozen people were kneeling before the crucifix, which had been placed with great ceremony on a coffee table cum altar. The rest were in the driveway and street, singing and listening as best they could. I knelt next to a doe-eyed woman holding a baby; she was rapt with the whole experience and bore a striking if unconscious resemblance to a pieta in a Christmas tableau. When the reading had ended, people began to move out. Don and I were among the privileged few who were presented with sampaguita flowers from the feet of the Christ. (They are still pressed into the book we bought from Leonora Pangan.) Rose made her way in to say goodbye and we were left with Dinah and members of the family that lived there, one of them being the old woman.

She invited us to sit in the dining room, which was very well furnished. Dinah served us large glasses of fresh milk with newly cut coconut floating in it. She explained that there would be a procession like this one every night until Easter (which was three weeks away). The crucifix and the statues of Mary, Joseph and various other saints would be rotated to different homes each night. Mrs. Rivera was first to receive the crucifix because she was parish elder, an elective position that apparently is a sort of lay priest.

While we rested and played with a darling little boy—Mrs. Rivera's grandson—we were told her inspiring story. Mrs. Rivera had been dying of cancer a few years ago, but she went to church every day until she no longer could manage it. It was about that time that "Tita Ester" had her revelation, and hearing about Mrs. Rivera's illness, went to visit her; she instructed her to get up and go to mass every day, no matter how bad she felt. Her son took her, difficult and painful as it was, and after only three days of masses, the cancer disappeared. The old woman has been in excellent health ever since, becoming active in the church, working among the congregation, and the year before had been nominated elder. We were impressed with what we had seen of this congregation—a beautifully integrated combination of Catholicism and Spiritualism. Their religious life centered in their homes, which was why the old Spanish church, which we had passed along the route of the march, was closed and dark.

Mrs. Rivera was thrilled to find out we are from

Chicago, as she has a son in Chicago who is—of all things—a doctor. He lives about a mile from us, so we were happy to comply with her request that we deliver some photos and letters to him when we returned. We asked her what he thought about her going to a Healer for her cancer—she said she had not told him. (So we told him and got exactly the reaction we expected: he did not believe us, rejected the whole idea of the Healers, and must have thought his poor mother had gone off the deep end and taken us with her. If it wasn't in his medical textbooks, it could not exist, period. But how do you question results?) By the time we had finished our refreshments—unfortunately not too satisfying as the middle class has an Americanized proclivity for overusing white sugar—it was 11 p.m. Mrs. Rivera's other son drove us back to the hotel, rushing in order to make it back home by curfew. Dinah, Mrs. Rivera and a couple of other people piled into the new Buick with us. The car indicated both position and money; this was a well connected family.

We were exhausted and thirsty, and besides, didn't want the evening to end. Novena means renewal and we had certainly been spiritually renewed. As anticlimactic as it sounds, we went to the Aurelio cocktail lounge for a beer rather than go to bed right away. We were so "up" anyway! A Filipino rock singer who played and sounded a lot like John Denver was singing "Rocky Mountain High" in the lounge. It was quite a paradox to the rest of the day, but we enjoyed it even more for being so—and almost didn't make it back to our own hotel by midnight!

ROAD TO BAGUIO

We wanted to see both Blance and Alex once more before leaving town and—typical tourists running short of money—we had to get a check cashed before we could get underway to Baguio. (Originally, we'd planned to take care of that errand the day before, but that was Bataan Day, a national holiday, so the American Express office as well as most other business places had been closed.) Joe Bush, the Mortons, and Don's parents had already flown up to Baguio while we were seeing Mrs. D. and Virgilio. We and the Schmidts had decided to have Boykho drive us, not only to give us an extra day in Manila, but so we could see some of the countryside as well as having access to a car for the rest of the trip.

Pat followed us to Blance's; we planned to drop her off at Mrs. Mendoza's home after we'd seen the Healers. Blance told Pat basically the same thing as Virgilio—that she could walk again with a few weeks of daily treatments. He did take a lot of infected matter out of her legs with a spoon, much like what he'd done on Jack's hip. She seemed disappointed, but we figured if she saw Blance, Virgilio and Alex every day and did whatever they asked (in short, really made an effort), she'd have a good chance at recovery. Boykho had arranged for his brother James to drive Pat around while we were in Baguio and make sure she got to see whomever she wanted as often as she wanted.

The next stop was Alex's. Don had to carry Pat up the steps to the apartment complex because they were too steep and narrow to accommodate the wheelchair. Ironically, Don was under orders from Alex not to do any heavy lifting, as part of the treatment for the urinary infection. But Boykho was too small to do it, and Chuck, who met us at the car, claimed a bad back, so it was up to Don to help out. Alex signalled us to bring Pat right up to the table, where he, like the other Healers, removed some clots and gunk from her legs and spine. Whatever the Spirit was guiding these Healers, it was sure telling them all the same thing in Pat's case. Sometimes they tell a patient different things and give varying types of treatments. Either way, it is best to listen and do what they all say, since they're working together—consciously or not—and using the same Source. Some of Alex's helpers lifted Pat into a chair at the side of the room to watch, and wait for the rest of us, after Alex was done with her. Of course, he also wanted to continue treating her for several days.

Alex took Don into the back room and blew energy on his fingers, explaining that it was a way of increasing Don's healing ability by transferring some of his own power.

Then Alex performed four quick operations on me in succession, taking out some blockage behind each ear, and from my ovaries. The total time was about 10 minutes. His instructions to me: not to wash any of the places he had worked on for three days. That kind of order is usually as much for a patient's self-discipline as for medical reasons in that it tests your will power and your sincerity in seeking help from the Healers. So we tried to obey as much as possible—but it was a ghastly thought in that heat!

By this time it was 10:00 and time to get Pat to Mrs. Mendoza's. Chuck walked us to the car and we told him Pat was going to be seeing Virgilio. He informed us that Alex and Virgilio used to be good friends, and that Alex had actually taught material healing to Virgilio, but from a source closer to Virgilio, we later heard it was the other way around —that Alex had studied with Virgilio. Whatever the truth was, it explained the similarity in their techniques. Unfortunately, jealousy from one or the other apparently interferred with the relationship, for they parted ways and each set up his own practice.

Mrs. Mendoza lives on an estate in Quezon City, with several buildings surrounded by a high wall, and a beautifully manicured lawn. We got Pat settled in (how delighted she was to find that the entrance to the bathroom was level and wide enough for the chair, which had not been the case at the hotel) and were offered something cold, sweet and fruity to drink—Tang! The Philippine upper-middle class is really Americanized, and the poorer for it in some instances. Virgilio wasn't home, but our hostess showed us his living quarters, consisting of a small, bare room in a guest house behind the main house, furnished sparsely with a cot, dresser, and crucifix.

It was noon before we finished our business at American Express (they'd allowed Don to cash a personal check there because he's a card holder) and made it out of Manila and onto the Kennon Road, the only highway to Baguio. It's two lanes and somewhat dilapidated, having been built by the U.S. Army Corps of Engineers long before World War II. Baguio is about 250 miles north of Manila, through the agricultural lowland provinces and into the mountains of northern Lujon. Pangasinan Province, where many Healers work, is about ⅔ of the way up from Manila, making Baguio our best headquarters for seeing both them and the ones in Baguio. (Now there are some resorts on the China Sea coast of the lowlands which are also conveniently located for tourists seeing the Healers.)

We thought there would be some relief from the tropical heat once we got out of the city, but we thought wrong; it was even hotter on the flats north of Manila. There were five of us in that little Toyota Corolla—the Schmidts, Don and me, and Boykho. It was crowded and sticky but nevertheless we were having fun, between being with friends and being filled with a sense of adventure! The land gradually changed from urban sprawl to swampy rice paddies and stubby remnants of the last sugar cane harvest. Our fellow travelers on the road included natives in coolie hats riding water buffalo, looking like a picture postcard from anywhere in southeast Asia. We passed by Clark Air Force Base, and just north of it, the Philippine version of Service towns everywhere, a sort of poor man's Las Vegas of clip joints, country-western dives, and souvenir stands. It represented the worst of what the U.S. brings into foreign countries willing to pay the price for our brand of prosperity and military security. Boykho told us this was an area in which the Huk guerilla movement had been strong prior to martial law. We could understand how the natives might resent such Americanization and allow the communists to operate.

We were getting hungry. Boykho knew a restaurant about a half hour up the road and it turned out to be a good recommendation. Not fancy, but clean, with those large ceiling fans that reminded me of "Casablanca" or something. The food was cheap and excellent: huge plates of Chinese steamed rice and vegetables, and boiled beef in sweet-sour sauce. And water with real ice, not easy to get in dry season in the lowlands! Then I asked the waitress where the washroom was and got a blank look. Boykho suggested I say "comfort room." To tell the truth, that was a better word after two kidney-jogging hours in a car with weak shocks on a road that hadn't been repaired in decades. While we were eating, natives kept walking up to the door and windows to peer in at us. They were curious as to what we were doing there, I suppose, for we didn't seem to be Air Force types, but they rarely saw any other Americans, since most tourists go to Baguio by plane, train, or express bus. One man on a water buffalo rode right up to the door to get a good look. Mary Ann snapped his picture, and he tipped his hat. How nice to be traveling in a foreign country where they still like Americans!

Back on the road, we passed through tiny hamlets of thatch-roof houses built up on stilts. Building them off the ground makes them cooler, and affords protection from animals and from flash flooding in rainy season. The only way to tell who was the richest person in a village was by counting the livestock—pigs and chickens ran about freely in the yards, and there was an occasional cow or water buffalo. Coconut and pineapple trees line the road, but beyond that there was little vegetation. So rural, but in every town were the inevitable signs of American influence—advertisements for Coca-Cola and Kodak!

We were making pretty good time. It was about 3 p.m. when we came to the archway over the road that

welcomed us to Pangasinan Province. We were beginning to get into gently rolling countryside, with
volcanic peaks visible at a distance. We'd already
passed through the villages of Carmen-Rosales and
Urdaneta before the names rang a bell as being
hometowns of some of the Healers. When we realized
it, we turned around. We decided to take advantage
of the daylight to start finding out where they were.
But we would be in something of a hurry; we wanted
to get to Baguio before dark because the road is unlit
and treacherous at night. We had the addresses but
the streets were not marked so Boykho stopped and
asked a couple of people where we could find Juanito
Flores. (Nobody spoke English, so it was a good thing
he was with us.) After a couple of bum steers, someone directed us to a concrete building just off the
main road. It was Flores' chapel. No one was there,
but a neighbor sent us further down the road to his
home, where we met his mother. She told us he was
out working the fields that day but suggested we
come back the next day. At least we would know
where to go with little wasted time and effort.

We proceeded back south to Carmen-Rosales to
find Josefina Escandor-Sison. We had a terrible time,
backtracking and asking at least a half dozen people
how to find her. We finally were told to go past the
school, down a long dirt road where we jolted along a
couple miles of dusty wagon trail, past a cluster of
stilt houses, past water buffalo and goats tethered in
the drainage ditches. And we saw the strangest dogs
imaginable, half-starved mutts with pig-like noses.
Don was especially startled by them, so much so that
he gasped and excitedly ordered Boykho to stop the
car. It seems he'd been doing visualization exercises
for months before our trip as part of his psychic

development class; he tried and tried to visualize an ordinary St. Bernard, but no matter what he did, all he could get was these same weird black and white, snaggle-toothed creatures. Eventually, he gave up and just focused on them, and here they were in the Philippines, animals like something out of a dream, and yet we all saw them.

We finally managed to find the Healer's house. And Josefina—another person with that intangible quality that makes her so special. She was a little suspicious of us at first, until Boykho assured her we were not there to harass or ridicule her. But she would not work on us, because her Spirit Guide had told her to take a sabbatical the three weeks before Easter, then she was to have a vision of Christ on Easter that would increase her healing ability. Meantime, all she could do was tape an interview.

Josefina, like Alex, had prayed for years to be able to help people. But she specified wanting to be a Healer. For 11 years, she underwent physical, mental and emotional trials to be worthy, making all kinds of sacrifices—given to her in dreams—to attain the level of spirituality she needed to heal. For example, she would have to go for days at a time without speaking, or she would have to fast or go without sleep for certain periods. It worked. She began doing magnetic healing and one day was able to do material healing, removing the infection of a bad appendix. She is still in the same village she was born in. The house was very poor, quite a contrast to her own physical beauty. The tape with her is all the more interesting because of the sounds of chickens and ducks and pigs in the background. After talking with her, we could well believe that she deserves her reputation as one of the best Healers. ("God is an equal opportunity employer," according to my feminist friends.)

Once again heading towards Baguio, we saw a sign on a mailbox, "Jose Mercado," which had to be Mercado, another lowland Healer we wanted to see. It didn't look as if anything was going on there, so we didn't stop, because our tour was scheduled to see him the next day anyhow, and it was getting late. A sign on another house further along read, "Dr. Marcello Jainar," a Healer who works with Tony and apparently follows Tony's lead in encouraging the use of the strictly honorary title "doctor." (A lot of the Healers go by "Reverend" or "Brother/Sister" so-and-so, legitimately, as heads of the Spiritualist church; Tony has recently established a new church and pretentiously bills himself as its "Pontifus Maximus.")

We were awfully glad we had decided to drive to Baguio and to get a look at the "real" Philippines. But during the next leg of the trip we weren't too sure if it was worth it. As we entered Benguet Province, the character of the highway changed, at this point taking on the well deserved descriptive nickname, "Zig-Zag." The mountain peaks were close by now, and the road upgraded sharply, getting steeper and steeper as night began to fall; the air was thinner, and the car was grossly overloaded with all our luggage piled on the roof. Cars and trucks came barreling down from the direction of Baguio, their headlights affording us occasional glimpses of the bottom of rocky valleys far below. There was no guard rail in most places, and the road was virtually one lane. And this in a country where the drivers are suicidal anyhow, rushing around hills and speeding into blind curves. Needless to say, we were petrified.

Then all of a sudden the car just wouldn't take it any more. It stopped dead, then began to slip back, the motor sputtering. In vain, we tried to talk it forward but it wasn't listening. Boykho put on the emergency brake and we all piled out to the side of the road, hugging the inside berm and trying to watch for headlights. Don and Boykho adjusted the mixture in the carburetor and began to push the car uphill, past the grade where we'd stalled. After what seemed like an eternity, it caught. We got back in and chugged onward. We were literally sweating, but it was not from the heat; the night air in this part of the country is cool all year round, and by now we were driving with the air conditioner off and the windows open.

A few miles up the road, there was a government checkpoint where soldiers looked at our passports and at Boykho's birth certificate. We asked if there was any place to get a drink of something cold and they told us there was a stand a short way up the highway. It turned out to be a little booth with an ancient man and even more ancient pop machine. But there was no ice, and warm coke and orange slush just didn't cut it—what we really wanted was plain old water!

It seemed like we'd been driving forever. About a half hour past the roadside stand, we saw lights atop a hill, which Boykho said was our hotel, the Pines. It looked close, but that 15 miles would take us 45 minutes, which says something about the so-called highway. Boykho was attempting to be cautious but for the most part was driving like a typical Filipino—scaring hell out of the four of us.

As we approached the city, I was reminded of San Francisco, because of the similar climate and the lights from myriad homes scattered on the hillsides.

The resort city twinkled on a hundred slopes and valleys, for this was the time of year when the capital is moved to Baguio to avoid the intense heat, and most of the government officials are in their summer homes. We finally reached the Pines, sitting atop one of the highest hills overlooking Baguio City, at about 8:00. It was even more luxurious than the Filipinas (reportedly the Marcos family owns a substantial chunk of the Pines), its wood-panelled lobby glowing from a blazing fireplace that warded off the mountain chill. Rock music blared through the lobby from a States-style discoteque, and expensively dressed couples and teenagers strolled through the garden. We decided to eat, and ran into Don's folks and the Mortons in the dining room, so we had a nice little reunion. Things were better with them after our two day separation. We took a table next to them on the patio, near a multi-colored fountain, while Nate filled us in on what had been happening. While in Baguio, in addition to Tony, we were supposed to see Mercado and Marcello. Diplomat was sending a bus for us early the next morning to go to the lowlands to Mercado's. We decided it would be better if Jack and Mary Ann did not go with us, because of the previous mixup they'd had with the travel agency, therefore Boykho was going to drive them back down to see Flores, who was supposed to be good with bone problems such as Jack's hip.

Our room was a disappointment compared to the hotel in Manila. It was much smaller and did not have a double bed as we had requested when we'd made our reservations through the travel agent months earlier, though Jack and Mary Ann had reserved their room only a couple of days before and got one. We were a bit put out when the hotel people told us they couldn't do anything about it because the hotel was full up, but we were too bushed to argue or even to take the Schmidts up on their kind offer to trade rooms.

FLORES

Our first order of business the next morning was to demand a change of rooms. It wasn't supposed to be mosquito season, but the hole in our window screen and the bites and buzzing we put up with all night long told us the mosquitos didn't know it. So we packed and the roomboys said they would move our bags while we were gone. (They did—and much to our amusement, they moved the beds together in the new room without our asking.)

We ate breakfast with the rest of our group, then were picked up by the Diplomat mini-bus, with Tony's smart-alecky young cousin as guide. Then, down that hairy road towards the lowlands. Don and I had experienced it before, but Joe and Don's folks and the Mortons were having minor fits every time we had a close call, which was every time we neared any other vehicle. Even we were startled by one thing: we came around a curve, and there ahead of us was a monstrous face hewn in the black rock, a beautiful sculpture of a lion's head that looked as if it would swallow the car until we hit a bend in the road just before reaching its jaw. We thought it must be some exotic, ancient war god; it turned out to be the Baguio City Lion's Club war memorial!

We got to Mercado's about 10:00, and of course,

Diplomat had fouled up again—Mercado's wife informed us he would not be working for another four hours. The travel agency had conned us—not surprising based upon past record—into thinking they had set up a special appointment with Mercado, when all they had done was take us to what should have been one of his regular work sessions. Don and I knew we were very close to Flores' place, so we suggested all going over there first then coming back to Mercado's later. We'd been getting along fine with our gang since we got to Baguio, but they sure didn't like that idea. In fact, they seemed offended at our eagerness to toy with the itinerary, even though it was not working out. And to make matters worse, Tony's cousin told them Tony would be unhappy with us or something, intimidating them into being afraid to go see other Healers. So we would be on our own again.

We were going to wait for a jeepney or bus to pass by Mercado's and flag it for the short trip up the road to Flores' (perhaps two miles). I waited out by the road, sitting on the rail fence, while Don continued trying to reason with the others. The tour bus was going back into Urdaneta to kill time at a restaurant and would be passing right by Flores' place, so we decided to go with them. We didn't tell them we planned to jump ship—after all, we wouldn't if nothing appeared to be happening at the other Healer's—but we did keep our eyes open. We saw Boykho's car parked near Flores' chapel and asked to be let out, knowing Mary Ann and Jack would be there. We once again told the rest of them it was their money and their trip, and they could take advantage of the opportunity to see another good Healer if they wanted. Tony's snippy punk of a cousin talked them out of it again, but begrudgingly asked the driver to pull over and let us off. So the vibes were bad between us and the older members of the tour once more.

Flores' chapel consisted of a plain concrete block building with a raised platform inside, and two rows of wooden benches split by a center aisle. We sat down across from Jack and Mary Ann and watched the goings on for a few minutes, but we couldn't see what was happening on the stage. A woman in front of the stage was calling names out of a book, and these seemed to be the ones the Healer was working on. So we signed the book, then lined up for a spiritual injection. People ahead of us were actually jumping when Flores gave them the injection; when he got to me, I understood why: when he reaches into that Bible and zaps you with psychic energy, you really know it. First he turned me around a couple of times, placing his hands on my shoulders, and made a comment about how tall I am, grinning and standing on his tiptoes! Then he held up his forefinger and middle finger in a V and tapped the back of them against the nape of my neck. And I felt as if electricity were running through my whole body, like the static shock you get from a wool carpet in winter, but much stronger and more directed.

The woman assistant called out Don's name. Flores took a long look at Don's neck, still bandaged from where Blance had taken out the cyst. He ripped off the bandage, and we didn't have to understand Tagalog to catch the derision in his tone as he laughed and pointed at the cut. He was scoffing at Blance's inability to operate without leaving a scar, someone translated. (But it isn't inability so much as a difference in styles; Blance leaves the mark as a reminder.) However, Don was having some trouble with Blance's opening. His hair was growing back in and curling into the cut, keeping it from closing. Flores said it was getting infected and that he would close it up later on. He never did—but his probing of the wound caused it to start bleeding, and he didn't even rebandage it. Don was disgusted at Flores' arrogance. Why, oh why did there have to be this jealousy and cattiness among the Healers, whom we felt should be above all that? Still, we could feel that Flores is a powerful person.

While Flores was working on Jack's back and ears (magnetic healings and some clots removed), we went outside to get some fresh air, where we met a young couple from Vashon, Washington who told us their sad story. Joyce's liver and pancreas were riddled with cancer to such an extent that when she had exploratory surgery, the doctors couldn't even attempt to get rid of it. They just closed her up and told her there was nothing they could do, that she'd be dead within a year. They, like us, had been involved with the spiritual-occult field for a while and Tom, her husband, had done some spiritual healing. So they decided to give the Philippine Healers a try. They had nothing to lose and everything to gain by leaving their baby and business for as long as it would take to get Joyce cured. Flores and Mercado had each worked on her so far—and each had removed tumors of the exact description the doctors had given her of what was inside her, yet she had not told them what the doctors found. There was one huge mass on the liver, surrounded by seven smaller ones. The Healers had been working on the small ones but hadn't been able to do anything with the large one. Nevertheless, she felt confident she was getting a great deal of help, for the pain was already lessening.

Flores was taking a lunch break. An assistant came out to tell us to come back in about two hours. It turned out she lives in Chicago only a mile or so from us but works with Flores whenever she goes home to the Philippines. We've been to visit her and her husband and children several times, and they've given us many pointers on developing our own psychic abilities.

As it was about noon, we figured we'd better get something to eat. Boykho took us and the Schmidts into Urdaneta. There were two decent looking restaurants across the road from each other, so we opted for the one that did not have the Diplomat mini-bus in its parking lot. It was called the "Family Rendezvous." While we ate barbequed beef and pork, and drank excellent San Miguel beer, Boykho told us something very interesting. He was staying with a business associate of his father's in Baguio, and had told him how inefficient Diplomat Travel was and how disappointed we'd been in Tony. The man told him Tony's family owns Diplomat, which clarified things somewhat—such as why the travel agency people were giving us a hard time about seeing other Healers, and why they tried to push Mary Ann and Jack onto our tour. We found out later that Tony rarely works on anyone who does not come to the Philippines on his tour through his agency (whose prices are comparatively high).

We decided we ought to let the group across the street know what we had found out. The hard feelings weren't doing anybody any good, and it might help them see our point of view. Don went across the road. It worked; the air was cleared, the others were able to see how petty Diplomat was being, and why. And more good news—Nate had taken some initiative to make arrangements for our group to see Placido Palitayan, reputed to be a great Healer. It seems a man had come to the Pines the day before and asked Nate if they were seeing the Healers. When Nate said yes, the man told him he works with Placido, and set up an appointment. It sounded similar to, if not as dramatic as, the way we'd met Chuck Isaacs and been introduced to Alex. Don's delight was apparent when he returned to our restaurant to bring us up to date.

We got back to Flores' chapel well ahead of his 2:00 starting time to find that the others had gone on back to Mercado's. We figured we would try to catch him later, but we might as well finish with Flores first. We sat inside and looked around at the people, which included a smattering of Germans and Americans as well as the natives. The natives in the lowlands looked different from those we'd seen in the city (generalizing, of course)—they appeared more like American Indians and less like Spaniards than the urban Filipinos. There seems to be less watering down of the tribal bloodlines as you get away from the cities; the people are stockier, darker-skinned and have broader features.

The first operation Flores did after lunch would have made a spectacular film sequence, but unfortunately he does not allow photography, because he's had some bad experiences with cameras being distracting to either himself or his patients. An old woman was having stomach pains, we found out from Joyce and Tom's guide, who was translating what she heard up on stage. Flores poured alcohol on her stomach, then used the side of his hand to make the opening, in a slicing motion. It was kind of a cross between the slash technique of Blance and the massaging of Alex and Virgilio. He began pulling out some kind of material from her belly. We heard the word, "Witchcraft." We looked—the thing coming out of the woman was a large plastic cleaner's bag, soggy with blood and water. This was even more astonishing than the rope thing we'd seen at Alex's and even less easy to believe. Sleight-of-hand? Who knows? But the next operation was certainly not trickery.

Flores picked up the book and called my name, and I walked up on stage. He again gave me a once-over, which I sensed wasn't entirely for diagnostic purposes (boys will be boys), and wrapped me in a sheet from head to toe. I didn't say a word to him and I had not indicated in the book what I wanted done, though I was hoping he could help my monthly cramps. He circled around me on tip toes, like a cat, lifting the sheet away from time to time in spots. This was his "x-ray" procedure. He pointed to the table and I climbed up, calling for Don to come stand by me at the head of the table. Flores proceeded to work on my lower abdomen, first taking out what Estelita, the Chicago woman, said were fibroids. Interesting, as a gynecologist had recently told me I was getting them! I hardly felt anything, but a followup visit to a gynecologist proved the problem was solved.

Next, Flores poured alcohol on my stomach. I thought it had been heated, it felt so uncomfortably warm on my skin. But when he touched me and his hands were suddenly equally hot, I realized his Power was beginning to manifest so strongly there was actual heat energy produced. I really felt his opening this time. He was pinching and pulling something. I groaned. Don took my left hand and Estelita my right. I gritted my teeth, knowing it would be over in a couple of minutes, determined to grin and bear it. I felt a scraping that I thought was deep inside me. Several people gasped, including Don. I had my eyes closed, so only later did I find out exactly what he had done. Through a translator, Flores told me he was cleaning out my Fallopian tubes, which he said were clogged with sperm and egg cells from taking the pill. (Those tubes can get clogged up and there is a regular medical procedure for cleaning them out, but this bit about the pill was new—is there something we don't know about how it really works in some cases?) What I didn't know was that he had pulled my Fallopian tubes up away from my body and was using his fingers in a scissors grip to scrape the garbage out of their open ends into a dish. Don said his hands were at least 8 inches over me, but I felt that scraping and the nerves being pinched as if it were inside me. The people around me were able to see the opening clearly.

Estelita told me everything would be alright now, because now I could have a baby. I started to cry, as much from what I was hearing as from the pain. Gynecologists had told me for several years that I might have trouble getting pregnant due to the small size and tilt of my uterus. Estelita said Flores was doing a magnetic healing to straighten it out, and it worked—my next medical checkup, it was in an almost normal position. But the last thing I wanted to worry about at that time was having a baby. The ex-Catholic Filipinos assumed I was weeping with joy at hearing I was no longer "sterile." Well, it was nice to know things were normal, even if they didn't know much about family planning. Ironically, I was doing public relations for Planned Parenthood at the time!

I went outside and sat on a tree stump after Flores had finished putting everything back in place. There was not a mark on me, but I was very tender and shaky. It felt as though I were bruised inside. Joyce and Tom cheered me up with a story about a friend of theirs who'd seen the Healers—an incident that was humorous for its irony in relation to my situation if nothing else. This woman had asked a Healer to give her a checkup, and he told her there was something blocking her stomach, which he would take out. The Healers never remove healthy tissue of any kind, only things that do not belong in the body naturally. So he reached in and pulled out the IUD she had just spent $60 to have her doctor insert! We chuckled, then speculated: was it merely a lack of knowledge on the part of the Healer, or in this woman's case, was there a reason his Spirit Guide directed him to take out the IUD?

The subject turned to babies and childbearing. I asked out of curiosity if the Healers do deliveries. Joyce said yes, and also C-sections. But what about abortions—is there a moral or legal reason they don't do them, or do they? Joyce said they do not, but not for any religious reason. It's just that a fetus is normal, healthy tissue and they won't touch it, other questions aside. The Healers also don't usually interfere in the case of a baby with a birth defect, because those are most often karmic, but they have been known to help defective persons later in life, if they've advanced enough spiritually to dump that karma.

Flores did a quick magnetic healing on Don's

ears but made no further reference to Blance's opening. He also gave all of us he'd worked on certain instructions, more complicated and numerous than the ones we'd gotten from other Healers. We weren't to bathe those spots for five days (I still had two days to go on the same instruction from Alex and Virgilio, so it was only three additional days for me). For five days, we were to stay away from fruit, meat, sour foods, cold things, and anything fermented, including alcohol. That severely cut down on what we could eat and drink. But worse, Jack and I had each been instructed not to have sex for 36 days—Mary Ann and Don weren't overly thrilled about that one! It made sense considering what Flores had done on me, but how it would help Jack's hearing was totally beyond our comprehension.

Flores disappeared into the house in back of the chapel with some of his assistants. Don followed to try to see him about the open wound on his neck, but Flores, after keeping him waiting several minutes, sent word through a translator that he could not see him. All he did was give Don a bottle of coconut oil to apply, which Don felt was awfully arrogant and inconsiderate considering it had been his probing that had irritated the opening to begin with.

MERCADO

Boykho drove the Schmidts and us back down the road to see if we could catch Mercado yet that afternoon. He was still working, and our tour group was still there. We watched a few operations, none of which I remember well, because I was still a bit dizzy and in pain from what Flores had done, my stomach was upset, and I was depressed for some reason. I decided to return to the hotel with Boykho and the Schmidts. Don waited to come back on the Diplomat bus with the others. Basically, what was wrong with me was that everything was starting to catch up with me. Our schedule had been hectic and I was rundown. On top of that, having a lot of healings done in a short time can be a shock to the body, and even the slight blood loss can add up while the body's forces are trying to rebalance themselves.

Over supper (while I copped everybody's rice because I was starved and there was little else I was allowed to eat), Don told us of an incident that had taken place that afternoon at Jose Mercado's. He'd been standing in line for a spiritual injection, with an obviously skeptical American serviceman in back of him. They started talking. The man was married to a Filipino. His wife and mother-in-law had dragged him to see the Healers, and although he was amazed at what he had seen so far, he didn't really believe it.

Not yet. Then he got his "shot" of energy. And when he actually felt that tingling sensation, he literally jumped in surprise. He rolled up his sleeve, and much to his astonishment, found a spot of blood where he'd received the "imaginary" shot. Don said the look on the man's face was priceless. But that was only the beginning. He stood next to Don and watched as Mercado performed several material healings, obviously authentic. He turned to Don, overwhelmed, and shook his head. As he walked away, he said, "Man, I sure got a lot of thinkin' to do!"

I use the story to illustrate what so often happens to a westerner upon first encountering psychic surgery. Even when your mind is not entirely open to it, you can not deny your eyes—even after dismissing anything that could conceivably be sleight-of-hand; and you can not deny results. This man realized he would have to reshuffle a lot of what he believed in order to totally absorb the experience. He told Don he'd send us copies of the pictures he was taking, but we never got them. Sir, if you read this, let us hear from you!

Don was somewhat down that evening. He had so much hoped that Flores or Mercado would be able to take out the last lump, a calcium deposit low in the neck, all natural material and not really a growth. He went into town to find out where yet another Healer, Eleuterio Terte, could be reached. Boykho, Jack, Mary Ann and I talked for a while, and tried to call Pat in Quezon but couldn't get through. We—and especially Boykho, who had a crush of sorts on her—wanted to know how she was getting along. But the long distance service in the Philippines isn't too good, so we finally gave up. I went to bed, utterly exhausted, about 9:00.

THURSDAY MORNING—MARCELLO

Thursday already—and we were scheduled to leave for home Saturday. My abdomen was still sore, and I was still drained out in the morning, but I was afraid I might miss something significant if I stayed at the hotel. We were to see Marcello Jainar, a lowland Healer who works with and is said to have trained Tony; he would be working at one of Tony's homes in Baguio, so that is where Boykho took us. The rest of the group was coming later in the minibus, but we wanted to catch Marcello early so we could get to the lowlands again.

Tony's house is obviously owned by a wealthy man—all wood-panelled inside, and the design is American ranch-style. He has views up and down the mountain, with a Diplomat Travel advertisement on the front lawn. But the most surprising aspect was cages of beautiful fighting cocks on the front terrace. It seemed incongruous that a Healer would be raising birds for that bloody though popular pastime, but we were informed that's what they were. Don, always sensitive to things like that, kidded me about my aversion, because I used to be a Mexican-style bullfighting fan and had only recently begun to see the cruelty beyond its artistic merit.

Marcello was not yet in when we got there; he

arrived a half hour or so later via a jeepney from the lowlands. And he, too, had that special quality that would enable you to pick him out of a crowd. He was accompanied by an elderly Filipino calling himself "Grandpa" whose story is most interesting. Grandpa had been in a wheelchair for 35 years, and was totally blind. At the time, he was living in Las Vegas, Nevada. When he retired home to the Philippines, he decided he should give the Healers a try. Tony invited him to move into the house so that he and Marcello could treat him every day. Three months later, the old man was walking and his eyesight was restored. He was so impressed and grateful that he stayed on to assist the men who had helped him so much.

By the time Marcello started working, there were a number of people there: an American sculptor and his wife, an American woman from Hawaii, and a physician from Hawaii, as well as the rest of our group. Marcello was so late getting started, we knew we would have to forego the trip to Pangasinan; we wouldn't make it back in time for our appointment with Placido as we'd been hoping.

Marcello took people into the bedroom one by one. It was so small not everybody could watch, so we all took turns observing and shooting pictures. It was Marcello who finally got the last deposit in Don's neck, taking out the biggest piece of tissue I'd seen a Healer handle. He started by rolling up his sleeves and jamming the middle three fingers of his left hand into the back of Don's neck. Then he brought out this long, spongy hunk of red stuff. (Don said later he didn't feel anything at all and still isn't sure about what happened, or if the Healers would really bother with that kind of lump, so we wonder . . .) I was attempting to take films but was almost doubled over with pain. I forgot to readjust the focal length on the zoom and blew another spectacular sequence. Don saw what Marcello supposedly took out and raised holy hell with me. I left the room in tears. Grandpa had no idea what was bothering me, but tried his best to comfort me, and was he sweet. I was very nauseous, and finally vomited.

The doctor was a strange character. He was skeptical, but we at least had to give him credit for making the effort to check it out. And he was furious at something that had happened a few days earlier when he was on his way to the Philippines: some of his colleagues who knew what he was going to do had reported him to the local A.M.A. chapter. The medical society contacted him to tell him the whole thing was a fraud and that he might jeopardize his professional standing with several Honolulu hospitals by making the trip. He didn't even belong to the A.M.A. and that kind of thing, he declared, was exactly why! So he was not intimidated. But when his plane refueled at Guam, there was a telegram for him from the medical society, informing him that he should turn around and come home because Tony, whom he had been going to see, had been in jail for the past two weeks. That was nonsense, for we had seen Tony within the last week.

The odd thing was that the doctor was more skeptical now than when he had started out, after three days of seeing various Healers. It seems that his negativity was getting to them. First, he refused to admit it when he had seen anything reasonably convincing. Time after time, he would stand there watching operation after operation and refuse to reach a conclusion. He'd say things like, "Hmph, well, I think I saw what might resemble blood." So it got to the point that the Healers would ask him to leave just before doing anything really outstanding. There was no point in their having to contend with that kind of distraction while they were concentrating on healing. And that he could not understand; not being psychically oriented, he figured they had something to hide from him. Marcello had not asked him to leave during Don's neck operation, but Doc had coincidentally (?) left to have a cigarette a few seconds before and missed the whole thing. Doc finally admitted to us that he had not come out with an open mind, that he subconsciously had come out to disprove it. And he did—to himself, anyway. There was just no way he was ready to open up to it. Of course, there are doctors who readily admit much goes on even in the operating room that wasn't in their textbooks, and who are not closed to the idea of paranormal healing.

PLACIDO

It was another so-called "coincidence" that led us to one of the finest Healers: the cab driver who brought Don's parents and Nate and Marge Morton from the Baguio airport to the Pines overheard them discussing their experiences in Manila and mentioned their conversation to Doug Voeks, an American who works with Placido. It was Doug who subsequently went to the Pines to see if he could find the Americans who were looking for Healers, eventually running into Nate and setting up the appointment to see Placido.

Doug drove to the hotel to pick us up but we needed a cab for the extra people, so we phoned from the front desk, and the driver on call turned out to be David, the one who had contacted Doug in the first place. We wondered if the Healers or their assistants ever ask the drivers to keep an eye out for groups like ours, and vice versa. On the way to Placido's, we found out a little about Doug. He had gone to the Philippines from his home state of Washington in January of 1972 just to check the Healers out, and was so impressed that he stayed until August studying with a few of them. He returned home for five months to settle things with his business and family, but could not talk his wife into moving to the Philippines with him, so they were divorced. When he came back, about a year after he'd first arrived in the Philippines, he met Placido, and has been working with him ever since. At first, he did the bookkeeping and answered American correspondence, things like that, then he began to do magnetic healing. By the time we were there, he could do material openings with Placido's hand guiding him. We got a letter from Doug shortly after we got back in which he reported he is now doing it on his own after all those months of patient study and personal sacrifice.

There were some other foreigners at Placido's when we arrived. (The weather is nicer in Baguio than in Manila at that time of year, and also the lowland and Baguio Healers are better known than the ones in the Manila area, which is probably why we ran into more tourists in our second week than our first.) Joanna, the woman from Hawaii whom we had met at Marcello's, was there, and also an English couple named Lance and Pamela Mesh, who lived in London. Lance, an Australian, was a dental surgeon and Pam his nurse. She had cancer of the thyroid and had had several regular operations, each time losing a piece of the thyroid along with the tumors. The doctors had taken out as much malignancy as they could without completely removing the thyroid. Lance and Pam decided it was worth a trip to the Philippines to try to get rid of the remaining two tumors, one large one with a smaller one underneath. She was scheduled for further conventional surgery as soon as they got home if it didn't work. Placido had been doing magnetic healings to dissolve the last two lumps, being reluctant to take it all out at once. When he came out of the bedroom to greet us, he told us he was very tired from working so hard and would prefer that we not take any pictures that day, as he would need all his strength and concentration to work, and cameras might be distracting. (Placido does allow photography, but usually not until he is sure of the vibration and intent of the photographer, and then only if it won't be disruptive; Don did get some films of him working later.) Placido called people into the bedroom one or two at a time, while the rest of us waited on the benches along the sides of his living room.

The walls of his meager home were crowded with newspaper clippings about him and his work, in many languages. He's well known and respected, yet so poor he has no electricity or indoor plumbing. His motivation for being a Healer certainly isn't money! On one wall hung a plaque with an unattributed quote that sums up the Spiritualist philosophy: "Success of great men depends more upon purity of their hearts than upon the means of action . . . all suffering is due to ignorance of a way to unfold the divine glory which is present within the self."

I still wasn't at my best, so I wasn't going to have him work on me. When he called Dad in, Don and his mother went in, too. But Placido asked her to go back out, "Power today is weak. Negativity destroys." Mom had been negative in many ways throughout the trip, not intentionally, but being skeptical and not making any effort to really understand what it was all about. She didn't understand exactly what Placido meant, but it hurt her. She asked me for an explanation, which put me on the spot. I didn't want to tell her that Placido thought she was insensitive (after all, she is basically a good-hearted person, just not spiritually inclined). The woman from Hawaii bailed me out of this awkward situation; she's a very perceptive person and although she had not heard the entire exchange, she picked up the gist of the dilemma. She told Mom that Placido meant her nervousness and concern for Dad were negative emotions that might upset him or the Healer. I hope the glance I shot her was every bit as grateful as the one I had gotten from the woman I'd given moral support to at Blance's while her husband's leg was being operated on.

Joanna went on to tell us about a dramatic operation she and Doc had witnessed in the lowlands that morning, in which Mercado had a woman's stomach opened wide. But even after that, Doc remained negative, and Joanna said his bad vibrations were getting to her. I said I knew just what she meant, an oblique reference to Mom and Mrs. Morton who were sitting in the next room complaining about the Pines' beauty operators. Dad was out by now, and he mentioned that he was picking up bad vibrations from somebody. His use of our "psychic" vocabulary was somewhat startling, because he just didn't say things like that about people, but we knew he was referring to the two Marges, too. In the midst of all these miracles, they continued to be oblivious of anything but themselves. Nate understood perfectly. He turned to me and asked, "How are you going to handle this in your book?" I grinned and said, "Tell it like it is." He wished me luck. Later on, he related something to us that Placido had said to Mrs. Morton: you won't be healed until you learn to comfort others. She demanded an explanation, which only served to prove his point.

Placido asked me to watch him working on Don, saying he wanted my vibrations. Quite a compliment! Placido works slowly and deliberately, not doing any kind of showboating. He massaged Don's back along the neck and upper spine until it was open, then matter-of-factly took out his hands and let it close, dumping some blood clots into a bucket under the bed. The only thing out of the ordinary—for psychic surgery, that is—was that he let Doug do some of the openings, with his own hand resting on top of Doug's to supplement the power. Don mentioned later that when Doug opened him, there was more pain than with the other Healers. It hurt a little and the pressure was greater, apparently because Doug wasn't totally in tune with it yet.

I went outside to get some fresh air and was surprised to find it was sprinkling. David, the cabbie, was surprised, too, telling me he'd never seen it rain in Baguio at that time of year, as rainy season wouldn't even begin for a couple of months. While we stood there in Placido's yard, I saw what perhaps was one of the most poignant scenes of the trip, because of its truthful simplicity in pointing out cultural conditioning. In the States, kids learn a lot from TV. Who among us has not played doctor or at least thought about going into medicine after seeing a medical story or reading a romantic story about doctors? In Placido's yard were two small boys, watching Placido work through the bedroom window and imitating his every move—playing Healer. First one would be the patient, then the other. These children, one of them Placido's son, were growing up accepting the "supernatural" as everyday occurrence, because for them it is. They identified and fantacized about Healers the way American kids do with cowboys. Don, joining us outside, asked why I hadn't tried to get pictures of those kids. I'd thought about it, but I knew it would be spoiled as soon as I aimed the camera at them, so I let it go.

David told us something of great interest—that he himself used to be a Healer! He worked with Tony for a long time, he said, but had abused his power and lost it. He was being punished but hoped to regain the Gift some day. He had nothing good to say for Tony, claiming Tony had shafted him in some kind of business deal. We didn't want to make any judgements one way or the other. But Don was pleased when David invited him to meet with him and another colleague so they could show him something about how they worked. Whatever the whole truth was, it was quite a story and an intriguing offer.

That evening, we tried to call Pat again. Mrs. Mendoza said she had moved out of her house and was staying at the Sulo Motel in Quezon City. But they didn't have her listed. Boykho called his brother James to find out what had happened. It was as we had feared all along: living so close to Virgilio, she was having trouble getting away to see the other Healers. She was at the Sulo but had only registered that afternoon so they had made a mistake. We tried again and got her. Everything was going great. She was much more optimistic than before. Chuck and Alex were working on her; she was especially impressed with Chuck, and says to this day that she wishes she could have stayed to have him work on her more; she's sure he would have had her up and around eventually.

DAVID'S BOMBSHELL

David picked Don up after supper. Don came back a couple of hours later, deeply troubled as well as angry. Instead of giving him tips about healing, David blithely told Don that the material healing is all a fraud, done by sleight-of-hand, and that only their magnetic healing is authentic. He demonstrated, supposedly, how some of it is done, but he was awkward and clumsy, most unconvincing for someone who claimed to have fooled people this way for a living. He promised that if Don would come back to see him again Saturday morning, he'd show him more. We did not want to believe David, of course, but he had planted this seed of doubt in our minds. Yet we knew some of the things we had seen, like that stuff Blance caused to roll out of my eye, could not possibly have been done by trickery. And why would David have told us all that stuff about how he had the Gift for material healing and lost it, only to turn around and expose himself as a phony? It didn't make sense.

We phoned Chuck in Manila to see if he could tell us anything. We already knew from Alex and Chuck that the openings were not really necessary to effect healing, that there is a psychological benefit. That didn't mean the openings were not real, though. We'd seen too much that was convincing and felt too many good vibes to allow ourselves to be let down by this one man whose motivation was questionable. But we didn't want to be taken for fools, either. We felt somewhat better after talking to Chuck in one way; in another what he told us was equally unsettling: he thought the openings were real but that the material they take out is often materialized or apported rather than actually removed from the body. If that were true, the Healers were no less fantastic, but at the same time the phenomenon of psychic surgery was intentionally being misrepresented.

We were in a quandary, not knowing where to turn or what to think. Boykho sensed it and asked us what was wrong. We confided in him and he was a big help. David had told Don no Healers did any openings before 1962, when the Philippines first became a tourist country on a large scale, and that they did the openings only on foreigners. Boykho had seen them work one time when he was a teenager, though, long before '62. At that time, they were working only on Filipinos and had done openings. He reminded us that we, too, had witnessed many openings on natives. So David was obviously lying on that score. Besides, there are reportedly direct or indirect references to psychic surgery or something akin to it in the literature of the Kahunas in Hawaii, juju and voodoo medicine people, the Kaballa, and even Amerindian shamans. Maybe David was just spreading sour grapes because of his conflict with Tony, whatever the reason for it. The bizarre turn of events did shed a little different light on Tony's show-biz approach to psychic surgery: perhaps he was trying to counteract stories like David was spreading. We would have liked to question Tony about it, but he never did show up for any of the appointments we were supposed to have with him in Baguio. Instead, he stood us up and went to see his dentist and work on some people in Hong Kong.

DAY IN BAGUIO

We ate breakfast Friday with Joanna and an American pilot and his wife who were seeing the Healers. We were playing Devil's Advocate in questioning them closely about the things they'd done, although it wasn't a planned thing. The pilot was prone to terrible headaches, and also was bothered by a wound in his hip and back he'd gotten when his chopper was shot down in Vietnam. He didn't want to report these things to the airline for fear of being grounded. Neither did he wish to endanger the lives of his hundreds of jet passengers. He knew about the Healers from flying to the Philippines all the time so he thought he would see what they could do, a few weeks before his annual company physical. So far, he said, they had removed some metal fragments from the war wound that the doctors hadn't gotten out, were restimulating circulation in that part of the body through magnetic healing and massage, and had gotten rid of his headaches completely. He felt much better and was thoroughly excited about the Healers, yet he was afraid to talk much about it or allow his name to be used for fear of repercussions from the airline or the Air Force reserves.

We invited Joanna to come with the Schmidts and us to look up Euleterio Terte, the Dean of the

Healers and the founder of the modern Espiritista movement. He's semi-retired but does work weekends at his home village in Pangasinan and sees anybody who is able to find his Baguio home. Don had traced him through his last known address in Baguio, at the back of his daughter's dress shop downtown. His house is high atop a hill overlooking Baguio. Jack, limping terribly, had a great deal of trouble negotiating the 50 or so slick, narrow flagstone steps; we admired his pluck for even attempting the climb.

Terte's lovely teenaged granddaughter answered the door, and told us to wait for a few minutes. We sat and watched a tank of tropical fish he had in the front room. In a few minutes, the wizened, tiny old man came out and introduced himself, still vigorous at well over 70. His Gift and spiritual attitude had not diminished with time or age, apparently, and his chiseled face was so interesting I couldn't stop staring at him. He spoke little English, but the girl handed us a leather folder that contained his life story and personal papers translated into English.

Terte's father had been a Spiritualist minister and had started the forerunner of the Espiritista in 1905. But the son did not become a believer until he was 30 years old, when he had a dream in which angels appeared to him and told him to heal. So he started practicing magnetic and spiritual healing. It was many years and much suffering before he could do the openings. For example, he had been involved with the anti-Japanese underground in World War II, and was a POW of the Japanese. After several years, he found he was able to do openings, but only by using a rusty knife. This was in the days before the Philippine government recognized the Healers, so he spent some time in jail for practicing medicine

without a license. That was all over now; he showed
nothing but the strongest and most positive emotions
and vibrations, not a spark of the arrogance or jealousy that occasionally reared its head in other Healers, and no resentment over his tribulations.

But we had to know more than what was on
those papers, so we asked for some hints on how to
improve our own abilities. He suggested Bible
reading, particularly John 15, 16 and 17, and Psalm
119. He also told us most of the Healers practice
yoga-like deep breathing. He said one thing that
seemed to conflict a bit with what Alex had told us.
Terte said a person must have faith to be cured,
whereas Alex said he had enough faith for both himself and the patient if the cure was meant to be. But
that wasn't mutually exclusive; it merely means that
the non-believer has come to a point in his or her life
where he can open up spiritually and be cured, by his
own free will.

Then Terte invited us to watch him work, and
asked for volunteer patients. He began with a magnetic healing on my eyes, first opening the window to
"chase the negatives out and up the hill." While he
put energy into my eyes, he went through the motions of shooing something out the window on the
breeze. My eyes seemed a bit less foggy when he was
done, but I had not felt anything at all. He asked for
a glass of clear water, which he set on the table while
he did magnetic healings on Jack's eyes and ears. He
appeared to be pushing energy into one side of Jack's
head and pulling the negative energy out the other
ear. What he "took out" he threw down towards the
water, which slowly changed from crystalline to light
pink to rosy to deep red. Yes, we have seen magicians
do something much like this, but it was also similar

to the water ritual many white witch covens go through when they perform a healing circle. He directed Joanna to lay on the bed so he could take something out of her stomach, doing a classic style of psychic surgery. All this time, the young girl had been singing and chanting a Christian benediction in Tagalog, which we got on tape.

But all the while, the specter of David's doubts hovered over Don and me. Jack and Mary Ann noticed we were exceptionally quiet, but we didn't let them in on it, as Jack was impatient and pessimistic enough without making him share this burden. He hadn't gotten the amount of help he'd hoped for and had virtually given up. We knew that some of the things we had seen could be "magical" effects, even the thing with the glass of water; however, we could not conceive of Terte stooping to magician's tricks. And though there might be fakers who tried to duplicate what the Healers do just to get money or attention, they could not duplicate many of the kinds of things we saw; they could not duplicate the feelings and psychic experiences we underwent around the more spiritual Healers; and most of all, they could not get the same results—the remarkable improvement shown by Don's dad, for example, who was such a skeptic that his cures could in no way have been 100% psychological.

We decided our best bet was to get away from the whole thing for a while and get our perspective back. Boykho accompanied us to a double feature movie in town—two martial arts films which turned up a few months later in the States under new titles and started that movie craze. They were a little too bloody for my taste, not emphasizing one bit the all-important mental and spiritual aspects of such disciplines as karate and kung fu. But Don, a sometimes student of the martial arts, at least imbued me with some appreciation for the skills.

That evening, all of us went to the city market, a kind of trade fair cum carnival on the Baguio village green. We played bingo, bargained for souvenirs, and even had our palms read by a pseudo-gypsy fortune teller whose obvious charlatanry made it all the more fun. She told me I'd be married five times, have lots of money, and be in danger in a car the next day, which, it turns out, were the exact same things she told everyone else. We ran into Tom and Joyce, who were getting a little discouraged, because in the two days since we'd met them, no one had been able to take out the largest tumor, though the small ones were gone. They had decided to look for help down in Manila so I gave them the addresses of Blance, Virgilio and Alex. We never did hear what the results were, and my letters to them have not been answered.

I didn't want the night to end—it was my last in the Philippines, at least for this first trip. Boykho was going to drive the Schmidts and me back to Manila early in the morning. Of the original Chicago group, only the Mortons and I were returning on schedule. The Mortons had already flown back to Manila, but Don's dad and Joe Bush were making slow progress and weren't about to give up in the middle of it, and naturally Don's mother would stay with his dad. I didn't want to leave, either, but had professional obligations to meet at home. I was alright until Joanna and Joyce each called our room to tell me goodbye. Then I broke down and cried, knowing how much I would miss Don in this, my first real separation from him since we got married. (And it would be less than a week, for heaven's sake!) But as much as that, I did not want to leave the Philippines and its people—I felt so at home and had so much to learn there.

DEPARTURE

Boykho, the Schmidts and I left the Pines right after curfew lifted, about 4:30 a.m. to go to Manila. Don rode with us to the lowlands, planning to see whatever Healers he could before taking a public bus back to Baguio. We felt bad in a way that Jack and Mary Ann had not decided to stay on, for Jack most likely would have gotten more help if he hadn't lost hope, but I was glad for the company. We all stopped for breakfast at the "Family Rendezvous." I tried to keep the tears back, but I am such a cry-baby, it sure wasn't easy. We dropped Don at Mercado's about 7:00, though he had no idea how long he would have to wait for anything to start happening. We had an uneventful three hour drive back to Manila, mostly sleeping, listening to Filipinos singing '40's and '50's American hits on the 8-track, and to Boykho's impossible dreams of coming to Chicago and making enough money as a cab driver to buy himself a coconut ranch.

We had several errands to run before 2:30 p.m. when we had to be at the airport. First, we stopped at the Khos' for Boykho to drop off some strawberries he'd brought from their friends in Baguio. Don had presented Boykho with his crazy white straw "Al Capone" hat as a parting gesture and Boykho's 16-

year-old sister grabbed it off his head to try it on. It was fun seeing the Khos once more, so we stayed long enough for a snack. Boykho had promised me we could stop by Mrs. D.'s to say goodbye, but before that we picked Pat up at the Sulo so she could see us off. She reported she had feeling in her legs and some control of her stomach and chest muscles for the first time in two years. (Unfortunately, that is as far as it went because she had to return home after only three weeks of treatments, and the exercises the Healers told her to keep doing at home were not as effective as they might have been had she stayed there. Sometimes those long term, serious problems can take a while.) I was afraid we would run out of time and I'd have to miss Mrs. D. but Boykho assured me he knew exactly where it was and that there was plenty of time to eat lunch first. The others voted with him, selfishly I thought. Or was I the one being selfish? I was uneasy all through lunch, not even very entertained by the lovely water ballet in the Sulo pool. I was right. We couldn't find the house for anything and finally had to give up and head for the airport. Neither Don nor I saw Mrs. D. again.

Boykho had to let us off in front of the main terminal due to that law about unauthorized people not being allowed inside. As he unloaded our suitcases off the luggage rack, I leaned over and kissed him on the cheek. He was embarrassed but pleased. I was still fighting tears when I told him goodbye and gave him a couple of messages for Don. They finally started coming down when I found out Diplomat had done it again: my name was not on the passenger list nor was my ticket waiting for me at the checkout counter as they had promised. Don and his folks were on it—the agency had gotten it backwards who of the

Sladeks was staying and who was returning to the States. To top it off, Diplomat was not listed with Philippine airlines, so I had to beg Nate to rummage through his suitcase for their phone number; he wasn't too happy about it because the bag had a broken lock which he had rigged with a paper clip and he had to tear it apart. Can't say that I blame him—he had to redo the whole thing while standing in the customs line.

While I was running back and forth between various counters, phones and airline offices, I had to carry all my bags with me. I finally paid a porter a few pesos to haul them. At long last, the airline got ahold of the travel agency, who said they would send the ticket by courier. It was at the desk at the Filipinas (which was where Don was supposed to pick his up later in the week—they sure got things turned around), and got there with what should have been only two minutes to spare before takeoff time. In a way I hoped I would miss that damned plane and could go back to Baguio! I rushed like crazy up the stairs, through the health check, where I was held up in line by an American sailor who was having trouble proving his valid cholera inoculation. Vowing to put Diplomat out of business forever, I got to the boarding area just in time to hear them announce that a mechanical failure would keep the plane on the ground for at least another hour. I was so upset and exhausted that I actually drank a Coke and smoked a cigarette, both of which are on my list of "Never . . . well, hardly ever."

Eventually, they called the flight. It wasn't crowded at all, which was a relief because the plane coming over had been like a can of sardines. I didn't want to sit with the Mortons or the Schmidts because their incessant smoking would bother me, so I plopped down next to a young Filipino woman who was pregnant and sobbing. There was instant empathy between us. She smiled grimly at me, and I smiled back, but neither of us meant it. It turned out she was leaving her parents and homeland for the first time, to join her husband who'd just gotten a job in the States.

For some reason, the flight back seemed shorter than the one out. Perhaps I was more comfortable, perhaps I had more to do—such as getting my notes in order—compared to the state of nervous anticipation on the flight to the Philippines. And I was so tired, I slept a full eight hours, wakening only because we were landing in Honolulu. We had two hours there this time and the airport was fabulous by day. Jack and Mary Ann and I explored, took pictures, shopped, and ate brunch. We had to take our baggage through U.S. customs, too, but it wasn't as bad as it might have been. We stood in line for about 20 minutes while inspectors went through everything, piece by piece, asking what we had bought overseas, how much we had spent, etc. The only thing they really questioned me about was my Japanese-made camera, but the case was so beat up I had no trouble convincing them it actually was three years old. And they did express some curiosity about the jar of coconut oil with the sampaguita in it, from Mrs. D.'s; it was a bit unusual and they have to be careful about drugs, etc. coming in.

We had left Manila at 3:30 p.m. local time Saturday afternoon, and after traveling about 20 hours, arrived in San Francisco at 7 p.m. local time, same day. We had a four hour layover to get our planes East; I wondered why there were no earlier flights between San Francisco and Chicago at mid-weekend, since we'd just missed the 7:30 one by the time we un-boarded and got ourselves together. I was scheduled for a TWA flight—and wouldn't you know, there was some kind of problem and it was cancelled. American and United each had a flight going out at midnight, so they fought over who would get us (me and the Mortons, since Jack and Mary Ann were booked on a Minneapolis-bound plane). American won by finding us first. While Nate watched our luggage, I ran all over that huge terminal getting our tickets changed, and what an enormous amount of red tape that was! We were on a Philippine Airlines tour package, so we were supposed to use an airline that had a reciprocal deal with PA. Neither American nor United did, but theirs were the only flights out, so I had to get the new tickets stamped by both PA and TWA, who did.

The Mortons were meeting friends for dinner at an airport hotel. Jack and Mary Ann and I settled down with coffee, corned beef sandwiches and new paperbacks. It was actually relaxing—if a bit of a bore—to just do zilch for a few hours, having run around like the proverbial headless chickens for two weeks.

Jack and Mary Ann's plane was leaving a little ahead of ours. I tearfully waved them down their ramp then met the Mortons at our boarding gate. I sat with them on the flight home only because there were no seats left in non-smoking. It was a very un-comfortable four hours but I actually enjoyed kicking over the whole adventure with Nate and Marge; she seemed to have mellowed somewhat and was con-fiding some of her problems to me. And there was this darling couple in front of us, an American air-man taking his Okinawan wife and their baby to meet his family in Wisconsin for the first time.

We encountered some rough weather and even I, flying buff that I am, was glad to hit terra firma at O'Hare at 6:00 a.m. I grabbed a cab to my grandparents' apartment, where Don and I had left our car. To my pleasant surprise, my father was in town visiting them, which took a lot of the edge off an otherwise lonely return. And did that strong American-style coffee ever taste good!

I drove across town on the almost deserted Sunday-sleepy streets. When I got home, I took a real shower for the first time in weeks. Thank heaven, the time had run out on the Healers' limited showers rule just a few hours before! I crawled into bed and slept for 24 hours straight. For me, it was over, yet only the beginning.

MEANWHILE, BACK IN THE PHILIPPINES

Don had to wait at Mercado's for several hours after we dropped him off, with nothing to do and nowhere to go. It was dreadfully hot by about 9 o'clock. About 10, Lance and Pam drove up in an air-conditioned car, so Don hooked up with them for the rest of the day. Don was supposed to have gone to David's at 11:00 a.m. but after much debating, and tossing and turning all night, had opted to go back to the lowlands instead. He figured that in Pangasinan, he could investigate psychic surgery all over again with a more objective and critical eye, then deal with David's allegations later. He wanted to settle the question to his own satisfaction rather than take David's word; he figured it would be better to avoid such a negative atmosphere while trying to search for the truth.

Apparently he made the right decision. Mercado worked on Pam, taking one of the remaining two tumors out of her neck. He had told her exactly what she'd heard from the doctors—that there was yet another full tumor left, and the beginnings of a third—although she had not filled him in on the medical diagnosis. He asked her to come back the next day so he could get out the other tumor, for like most Healers, he didn't do much on a single patient at one time. When he took the first one out, Don was watching very closely, not taking pictures, because he wanted to see everything clearly, without the camera lens. And when Mercado was through and took his hands away, the opening did not close up instantly as was normal. It was as if Mercado was reading Don's thoughts about wanting absolute proof. The few seconds that it stayed open allowed Don ample time to really see well into Pam's neck and ascertain that the psychic surgery had indeed been authentic. Lance asked Mercado if he could have the tumor, but Mercado wouldn't give it to him.

There was an operation on a tourist woman's stomach that was highly evidential, too. As soon as Mercado opened her up, some smelly pus ran out over her abdomen and onto the table. The Healer worked on her for several minutes, getting rid of that putrid infected tissue, whatever it was. The stench was awful until she was closed up again.

After that, Mercado took some material out of the front of Don's neck, while Lance took the films. Don felt Mercado rubbing underneath his chin. He heard a little popping and felt a trickle of blood. At the same instant, an odor assailed him, and Mercado pulled out a clump of foul-smelling mucus. Now Don was really glad he hadn't gone to see David. All David could have done by his inept sleight-of-hand demonstrations was sow more doubt without proving anything; but what Mercado had done that morning could not possibly have been faked. Now he was surer than ever that the whole thing with David was a test.

Don ate dinner with Joyce and Tom, who had just about decided to go home instead of going to Manila. They were discouraged and Joyce did miss their little girl. But Don gave new encouragement by telling them about Placido. They all went to see him after supper. Placido took out a small piece of the big tumor after examining Joyce carefully, telling her it was too much to remove all at once, but if she would come back the next day, he could take care of it. They were elated, of course, and Joyce and Tom vowed again to stay until Joyce was well. The next morning—Sunday—the three of them returned to Placido's, doubly excited because this was the day he had promised to cure her. But it did not work out quite like that. Upon checking her again, Placido realized that there was just too much cancer to operate on; he literally did not know where to start. He did assure her that he could dissolve the tumors with a series of daily magnetic healings, but they were understandably disappointed.

Lance and Pam had better luck in the lowlands. They went back to Mercado's as he had suggested. And he took out the second of the thyroid tumors, as he had said he would. That left only the small slivers of the newest growth which he said he would get rid of the next day if they came back yet again. But they were leaving the next day, so they decided to give Placido another crack at it, arriving while Don was still there. And Placido was able to take out that last bit of cancer. Lance had brought along a small bottle of formaldehyde in hopes of getting an analysis of some of the tissue taken from Pam. Placido willingly handed him the tiny pieces of tumor. They wrote to tell us what happened. The analysis had been done at a prominent London hospital by a pathologist Lance's doctor uses. It checked out: the tissue was the type normally found in the human pharynx, and was judged hyperactive. The pathologist was puzzled, though. How had they gotten ahold of a tumor so unusual as to not have any healthy thyroid tissue surrounding it? Was it some new surgical procedure which could leave healthy tissue intact while removing cancer? They said he was even more puzzled, as well as fascinated, after they explained it! Pam is fine now and it has been some three years with no recurrence. The only abnormal thing is that the doctors didn't leave much of her thyroid, so she does take compensating medication. Lance used to suffer severe and frequent migraines, but no longer does. They, like us, were very impressed and uplifted by the experience. (See Appendix.)

Placido worked more on Don, too, taking out additional blockage in his neck. For one operation, Doug did the surgery, getting Don's neck open without too much difficulty, but strangely, he could not get the spot closed back up without Placido's help. It left a little scar and red mark, which Placido said would go away in two or three days. After 24 hours, the scar had disappeared and after 48, the redness was gone, as he had said.

Placido also coached Don some on how to develop his own healing ability. There was such a good rapport between Don and Placido that when Don got ready to leave, something drew them into a big bear hug. Don had about $30 left and handed Placido $20 of it. Placido, either because he liked Don or realized he was running himself short, tried to give it back, but Don wouldn't hear of it. Placido had done so much for him.

Don was in a quandary once again. Alex had promised him help with healing ability (and to drain his other ear) but they were supposed to have met Friday at Alex's place in Quezon, while Don was still in Baguio. Now he didn't know whether he should stay on in Baguio and see Placido again, or go back to Manila for his last couple of days. He decided he would go back to Manila, see Alex, and stay at the Filipinas one night, then come home Tuesday. So following yet another sleepless night of wondering if he had made the right decision about something, he hopped the bus to Manila Monday morning. It was a miserable trip. He was unhappy and unsure to begin with, plus the bus passed by the lowland Healers' places, making him feel sadder. And the only stop was at a dumpy cafe that just missed being Americanized, but wasn't Filipino enough to be considered charming orcolorful.

The accommodating bus driver dropped Don on a street corner where he said cabs were plentiful so Don wouldn't have to go all the way into downtown Manila, but it took him 25 minutes to find a cab. He checked in at the Filipinas, and collected the suitcase we had left in storage there. He couldn't reach Boykho until suppertime. When he did, Boykho delivered a disappointing message from Alex—he was out of town on retreat and would not be back in till Thursday. So it was decision time again. Should he wait until Thursday and see Alex? If he did postpone his departure another two days, should he go back up to Baguio in the interim? He was tempted to extend his stay, but that meant he wouldn't be able to take a vacation with his son in August. He would just have to go home.

He and Boykho spent the evening with Pat, having taken dinner of American-style hamburgers to her in her room at the Sulo. He was totally depressed at the thought of this being his last night in the Philippines. I know the feeling.

Boykho was going to take Don to Mrs. D.'s to say

farewell, but it was not necessary. While Don was outside the hotel getting his shoes shined by a sidewalk vendor, Dinah drove up. Mrs. D. had sent her with religious medals for each of us, and small plastic-bound books with the Novena service in English and Tagalog. It was one more proof of Mrs. D.'s psychic sensitivity; the last thing we had told her was that we would both be going home on Saturday, so how could she have known Don was still in town?

Don and Lance had done some chatting about investment opportunities in the Philippines, so Don figured he might as well check into it in the few hours remaining before the plane's 2:30 departure. He took a cab to the Stock Exchange in Makati, where a very polite man in the lobby answered his initial inquiries and directed him to the office of a broker. They were closed for lunch, so Don grabbed a bite at a little native restaurant, all the while still wondering if he should go home that day. Returning to the Stock Exchange, he found a scene like something out of a 20's movie. Our brokerage offices have everything on computer and ticker tape; this one had all the figures on a chalk board with runners frantically trying to keep it updated. Don purchased some stocks with a post-dated check, then contemplated his plight over coffee. (A familiar refuge—he spent the entire afternoon of our wedding wondering over coffee if he should go through with it! It's a good thing he did, for we are now convinced that this whole Philippine thing is one reason we met in the first place!)

Time was running out. He had Boykho drive him to the airport, giving him all his remaining pesos. He had only moments to spare before check-in time. And Diplomat had done it again. His name was not on the passenger list, nor was his ticket waiting. They sent the courier with it. The takeoff was delayed anyway, which Don took as an omen he should stay longer. He boarded anyway and decided half-way home that it was a mistake. He couldn't sleep at all. In his distress, he zeroed in on the wing of the plane, which was moving up and down a little; it took a while for him to realize it was supposed to be mobile. At first, he was convinced the plane was going to go into the sea. He didn't talk much to anybody on the way home. His folks took a different plane at San Francisco because his Dad felt so good that they had decided to stop in Las Vegas for a couple of weeks before returning home.

Don straggled in just in time to get dressed and get to his office. He was depressed and bedraggled. He was carrying the big suitcase he'd taken with him, plus another cheap one he bought to carry souvenirs. Its latch was already broken. He also had a once carefully wrapped cardboard carton with that lovely DaVinci's Last Supper wood carving, which had been a real pain in the neck to bring home, because every time he went through customs or the FAA check, they undid the package. That night, he told me about his wheeling and dealing. He'd bought 70,000 shares of speculative stock. I thought, 70,000: there goes our stereo, our TV, our new car. I must have had an alarmed expression on my face because he started to laugh—and informed me that the total purchase was about $400. Philippine stocks were so cheap, what could we lose? The price per share was barely measurable in pennies in America, and if one of those mines hit gold, or an oil well gushed . . . all the sooner we could get back to the Philippines.

EPILOGUE

Upon our return, Harold Schroeppel, whose psychic development class I was just entering, asked me, "In one sentence, what did you learn in the Philippines?" My answer was, "That there is no such thing as coincidence." That exchange provided me with one of the themes for this book. But it took me well over a year to actually write it, for a couple of reasons. One is that I knew how difficult it would be to capture such a personal and subjective experience on paper, to fully share it. I kept putting off even trying, which is the second reason: I am a notorious procrastinator. Maybe it has also taken a long time to sort out the whole thing and put it into perspective. We returned full of missionary zeal, veritable fireballs of speech-making, film showing, and answering negative articles and letters in the media about the Healers. That has now been tempered by a few years of functioning in a different sort of world, in which skepticism is the key word, and tilting at windmills is frowned upon. And even that was good, for it allowed the chain of "coincidence" to continue until the timing was right and our understanding balanced enough to enable us to better determine what was needed in the book.

We met renowned occult author Brad Steiger

through our mutual friend, psychic Deon Frey, one time several years ago. When the first draft was completed, we felt we had nothing to lose by phoning him to see if he would look at it, give us some hints, maybe even write a foreword. He seemed to remember me and agreed to meet us, apparently wanting to ascertain exactly what our motives were. He must have been satisfied, for not only did he read the manuscript, he liked it well enough to put us in touch with one of his publishers, among the largest in the nation. They wanted it, sent me a contract for a healthy advance, and set a publication date; then, without warning, the editor remorsefully wrote that their legal department had found that a newly acquired medical publishing division would not allow them to print anything contrary to medical authority opinion. The critical atmosphere surrounding psychic surgery at that time—January, 1975—coupled with the faltering economy kept even the excellent literary agent Brad recommended from quickly placing the book with other publishers, because they would not risk a book by an unknown author, especially on that topic. The agent was confident he could sell it eventually; nevertheless, we were determined that it see print while the controversy was still on and the timing appropriate, even if it meant doing it ourselves. Brad was unfaltering in his support, promising to do the foreword under any circumstances.

We had acquired a copy of a favorable report from an international study done on the Philippine Healers in March, 1973, and decided we should contact some of the scientists and doctors involved. We tracked down the head of the group, researcher George Meek, at his Florida home in the fall of 1975, but he was reluctant to give out information because of plans to publish a book based on their five year examination of psychic healing around the world. (In a conversation several months later, Meek told us they, too, were having publishing difficulties, and consented to give us the names and addresses of his team members and other M.D.'s and scientists whom he knew had researched the subject.) He also reaffirmed that their study had found psychic surgery to be authentic, but he cautioned us that things had changed drastically since our initial trip, that there was a higher percentage of fakery, that many Healers were becoming corrupted by the publicity and money the whole thing was bringing. With that in mind, and because we wanted to get some new films—16 mm this time—Don returned to the Philippines for three weeks in April, 1976. He would find out firsthand about the alleged changes we'd been hearing of from George and others who'd been there since we were.

Unfortunately, it was for the most part true. To Don, the trip was disappointing to say the least, and to me, fielding his intense depression in several long distance phone calls (we couldn't afford for both of us to go back, but I could not do the filming), it was as if, once more, we were running an obstacle course. To the degree that things had gone smoothly and the timing had been flawless on the previous sojourn, everything went wrong on this one: cars that broke down, people who didn't keep appointments, problems with the camera and with getting cooperation in setting up decent angles and lighting, finding even such Healers as Alex with personal problems. In fact, Don wryly says that the only thing not changed was Boykho, except that he now has his family with him in Manila.

Some of the differences were puzzling—like Boykho and Don going out into the lowlands about a half a dozen times so Don could get some pictures of those weird dogs we'd seen before, and not spotting a single one in villages that a few years ago seemed populated by the creatures. Or talking to Mrs. D.'s husband to get the correct spelling of their name for the book and being told, "How wonderful. We didn't know you were writing a book," despite her having mentioned it to us three years earlier upon our arrival at her home. That did serve to reinforce our assumption that she's a true psychic, who often does not recall what she says while working on that level.

Some were really disturbing: catching Flores use a needle to give spiritual injections which didn't even feel like the electric type we'd experienced before; seeing Blance making an opening with a razor blade (though this does not mean he always uses one —perhaps only when the Power isn't coming through enough—and there was still almost no bleeding); an assembly line at Placido's that made his healing seem impersonal, much of it done by novice assistants.

And some were heartening, such as having the opportunity this time to watch the wonderful work of Josefina. Several reputable people had told us of seeing her put cotton in one part of someone's body and pull it out of an entirely different part. Don himself saw her stuff an exceptionally large wad into a patient and not take it out at all, saying she'd remove it the next week. Don is sure that wasn't faked: he was watching closely, and she, unlike many of the Healers, works with just her thumb and forefinger, leaving her hands wide open rather than in a fist. He also watched while Blance cleaned out some eyes, as he had mine—virtually impossible to fake.

So why would he, or any other Healer for that matter, perpetrate fraud on other occasions? We remembered the quote on Placido's wall that success is measured by purity of intent. Perhaps they feel that the end justifies the means, that if patients get a psychological boost to their cures by use of animal tissue or a phony opening, it doesn't matter that the Healers are purporting to be something they're not. Sometimes, too, when the Gift is just not there for one reason or another, the ego gets in the way of a Healer saying, sorry, can't do it today; or they don't want to let someone down who has come all that way to see them. But many of the newest of them are passing out business cards with the title "Psychic Surgeon," a term the other Healers never used. And it just does not seem right for even the real Healers to claim that what they do by apportation, materialization or especially illusion is psychic surgery, or that work they do on the etheric or astral plane that may effect a physical reaction is actually surgery on the physical body.

Sadly, these incidents of misrepresentation seem to be on the rise even among the legitimate Healers, probably due to increased notoriety and/or overwork. Plus, more people than ever who do not have the ability to heal are passing themselves off as Healers for financial gain. Yet many people still get good results. Although we can't vouch that 100% of what we saw even on the first trip was authentic, we saw enough of the real thing not to dismiss the whole phenomenon as quakery.

Blance's rolling a marble-sized piece of mucus out of someone's open eye, the type of operation we got on film during both trips, surely was not. But Don did catch him faking openings on the second trip. David Stewart, an Australian who was getting treatment for cataracts from Healers Joe Bugarin and Marcello Jainar while Don was there was not helped; they told Stewart they had removed the cataracts, but they were still present when he got home. In contrast, Nate Morton's cataracts really had been cured three years earlier. As for Placido, despite the change in the atmosphere at his new, more luxurious clinic, Don found him to be as warm, sincere and sympathetic as before—merely overworked. After all, when dozens of people come for help daily, what can he do but not help them at all, or train assistants whom he judges to have the spiritual capacity to carry part of the load? And the assembly line was no worse than waiting in a doctor's office.

Alex also was delighted to see Don again, and confided in him about some of the emotional upheaval his popularity as a Healer is causing him. (But Alex realizes what has been happening to him in the past few years, and was planning a three month sabbatical to put things back in perspective and renew himself spiritually.) There are just too many people who need help for all of them to get the same quality of care—the same problem hospitals are facing.

As in everything, there are two sides to the story. Would we still recommend that people go to the Philippines, make that arduous and expensive journey? By all means. But it is necessary to be aware of the hazards, to know what to expect, to be on the lookout for the phonies, and to see the human side of what the real Healers are up against. We do not condone some of their actions, however well-motivated, but neither do we think the good that they do should be overlooked.

Now, more than ever, we are not in a position to

convince anyone of anything. Our purpose is merely to expose people to our experience. We ask our audiences to hear us out with open minds then draw their own individual conclusions. Those who are ready to accept it will. Others who are already in the spiritual field may gain a deeper understanding. If someone doesn't believe us, we will not argue about it. Nor will we give people pat answers or tell them what we think they want to hear, or make up answers if we don't know something. We can't promise anybody anything. If what we say or do gives some hope where none previously existed, great. But no miracles take place for people who don't make an effort to help themselves, for example by searching out the best healers and really trying to understand their work, even though they may not agree with them. Not everyone who goes to the Philippines has the kind of experiences we did. People who lay back and look for the easiest path or make excuses will be let down. The Healers will not be able to give them a lasting cure for problems they should be working on themselves. Don's dad is a good example: he got so much help temporarily, then came back and continued to smoke and eat wrong and feel sorry for himself; within three years he was dead, despite the opportunity he had for his new psychic awareness to overcome his heart and kidney failure. The Healers can not be blamed in such a case, yet unfortunately, many people who should be helping themselves come home and tell others that the Healers aren't so terrific after all.

If we feel a person is not likely to get much help in the Philippines, we say so. To those who really want to go, we give as much information as possible, attempting to increase their chance of getting help, however slight that chance might be. We never push anybody one way or the other because people have to decide for themselves whether to take whatever risks might be involved in a trip of this type. Some go out expecting relatively little and come back mentally, physically and spiritually uplifted, while some are disappointed if they do not witness a series of absolute miracles. Every case is different, but the basic point is that nobody gets something for nothing. And for some, it is just too uncomfortable to throw out X number of years of pseudo-knowledge and fully accept the Truth the Healers offer.

And we are dealing in Truth, not only as we see it, but as various people do, from tennis champion John Newcombe, who was helped in the Philippines (see Appendix), to the scientists and medical people who concluded in the Meek-McCausland study that the phenomena connected with psychic surgery are genuine and real (see Appendix), to our various contacts worldwide who have sent us their own experiences. (See Appendix.) Regardless of the percentage of fakery or the percentage of misrepresentation by the real Healers, psychic surgery certainly must be closely researched for its fantastic potential and far-reaching implications. So far, it has largely been either actively denounced or virtually ignored by the very healing and scientific professions which should be most interested, instead of threatened. Perhaps parapsychological researcher/writer Ivan T. Sanderson said it best: "History shows that often the loudest skeptics are those who know nothing about the subject in question. They have not studied it and will not do so, for the very reason that they do not believe in it. Nevertheless they are prepared to take the time to pronounce judgement on it."

Jesus said regarding his own healings, "Except as ye see signs and wonders, ye shall not believe." (John 4:47.) That's what psychic surgery is really all about—tangible evidence of the omnific love and promise of that cosmic force in all of us that we call God. Because it is such an extraordinary phenomenon in and of itself, it's easy to lose sight of its underlying message—when we believe, having seen the signs and wonders, we realize that by serving and loving one another, we develope spiritually and become one with God, in tune with the forces of the universe.

APPENDIX

We originally had intended to draw on only our own Philippine adventure in this book, but because of the adverse publicity in the international media about psychic surgery and the changes taking place in the Philippines, we decided to add some supportive collateral material. We found that many people have had experiences closely paralleling ours. From their reports, we have taken a cross-section representing a broad spectrum: scientific and lay researchers, doctors (both medical men and Ph.D.'s in psychology), tennis star John Newcombe, the Meek-McCausland team, psychics, and others who, like us, searched out the Healers.

As with the entire book, the Appendix is not intended to be all-inclusive or conclusive, but it does utilize ideas and stories other than ours to give the reader further perspective on both psychic healing and the "supernatural" in general.

Pam and Lance Mesh

After we returned from the Philippines, we wrote to Lance and Pam Mesh, the London dentist and his wife whom we met in Baguio, to find out how they were. Not only did they report great results, but the letter includes the findings of the pathology report on the tissue Placido removed from Pam's cancerous thyroid.

Thursday, 7th June, 1973

Dear Marti and Don,

Many thanks for your letter. Nice to hear that you have both recovered from your operations, and that you have positive results.

We are pleased to report that we too have begun to feel much better. Lance is feeling dangerously healthy because he has not suffered from a migraine since his return. This is quite miraculous. Normally after a morning golf outing and a drink at the 19th, even if it was only a coke, Lance would come home with the makings of a migraine. As soon as he relaxed after a busy week's work, the old familiar thumping at the back of his head would commence. However, nowadays, he has been burning the candle at both ends—we have been extremely busy in the Surgery and our social life is just as hectic. Lance has been playing golf Sat. and Sun. mornings and competitioned for the club during the week, staying on for the social drinks at the 19th, we have entertained and been entertained until the wee hours, and other than the inevitable jaded head, no sign of a migraine. He feels as though he has been reborn.

As to my health—well, it seems to be taking a little

longer and I have had a couple bad days but not to be compared as to my previous 'bad' days. Before Mercado & Placido, I would have suffered for a much longer period, but I recover very quickly. It is only to be expected really, as the Healers cannot replace missing tissue, and I only have a little amount of thyroid left, just enough to keep me ticking over as long as I don't abuse myself.

As soon as we returned we had a professional photographer take a photo of the growth that we brought back in the fixing formalin. Later we gave the tissue to our G.P. who is also a personal friend. He in turn gave it to a Consultant Pathologist to do a histological analysis. We were very pleased with the report which is as follows:

Group Laboratory, Lewisham Hospital,
London, SE 13.
Specimen Received 30.4.73.

Nature of specimen:

Macroscopically 1. Piece of blood clot 3x1x0.5 cms.
2. Ovoid piece of tissue 3x1.5x1 cm on a connective tissue stalk 5cm stalk plus second piece of tissue 2x0.5x0.5 cms. Both pieces of tissue have greyish-white appearance on gross section.
Microscopically both specimens consist of smooth muscle fibres forming a thin wall with attached fatty tissue. The muscle fibres appear to be arranged in layers with ganglia of autonomic nerveplexuses between them suggesting an origin from the pharynx. There is a small collection of squamous epithelial cells present detached from the surface. There is no thyroid tissue. The history is unconventional, could it be part of a pharygeal pouch.   End.

The squamous cells prove that the growth came through the skin. Good evidence! So it was obviously hyperactive tissue. The Pathologist wants to see Lance and I to have a discussion re my unconventional surgery. I will send a photo over to you in my next letter. Sorry this one is rather grotty—my typing is only a two finger effort and I find the keys keep changing around. However, wanted to give you our report and post it off the first opportunity I had. The table is wonky the wind is blowing and I am distracted by the Patients—good excuse!!

We both send our Best Wishes

Pamela

Dr. Stanley Krippner, Ph.D.

*Dr. Krippner is a well known author and professor of psychology and parapsychology, currently Program Planning Coordinator for the Humanistic Psychology Institute and Director of Research for New York's Churchill School. He has also been Director of the Dream Laboratory of the Maimonides Medical Center, and president of the Association for Humanistic Psychology. This encounter with Josefina Sison took place while Krippner was in the Philippines in 1974 investigating psychic surgery, as described in his excellent book **Realms of Healing** (co-authored with psychologist Alberto Villoldo, and used with Krippner's permission).*

"I unbuttoned my shirt, spreading it out so far that nothing could be secreted in the folds. I also loosened my pants, lying down on the wooden table with my head on a Bible. Sison bowed her head in prayer and folded her hands. As she opened her hands, I could see that the fingers were wide apart. As the hands came down on my abdominal area, small red drops of fluid began to appear. Soon, streams of red fluid trickled down my sides. The fluid appeared to come from the part of my skin which came into direct contact with Sison's hands. There were no clotlike objects and she later took this to mean that the ailment was not serious.

"After wiping her hands and my abdomen with cotton, Sison tore a fresh piece of cotton from a roll and dipped it in coconut oil. Earlier, she had claimed that coconut oil was used by "psychic surgeons" for "healing" because "it helps direct the power of the Holy Spirit." Sison pressed the wad of cotton, which measured about one inch by half an inch, to the right side of my abdomen. While I watched, the cotton appeared to vanish into the skin until only a small tuft remained. As Sison gave this a pat, it also disappeared. Still standing at the right side of my body, Sison moved her hands to the left side of my abdomen. I looked at her hands carefully and they seemed to be empty. Again, the fingers were not pressed together and the palms were open.

"As Sison brought her fingers to my side, a piece of cotton appeared to protrude from my skin. She began to pull it up and I could see that it was streaked with red. I moved my body to get a better look. Sison stopped pulling, removing her hand from the cotton. And for that moment, the cotton appeared to be sticking halfway out of my body. Then she finished removing the cotton and I could see traces of red fluid on either side of it—but no coconut oil. She told me that the fluid was "impure blood" and that the coconut oil remained in my body to complete the "healing" process.

"Could Sison's effects have been the result of legerdemain? For this possibility to be considered, one would have to conjecture that small capsules of red fluid had been palmed by Sison before she touches a person's skin. The empty capsules would have had to accumulate somewhere—in the drawer of the table, on the floor, in her pockets, up her sleeves. However, Krippner, an amateur magician, reported:

"When I gave Sison a donation for her work, I noticed that she opened a drawer. It was quite empty, as she had run out of cotton, and I could see no capsules, empty or full. As for her clothing, she wore a shortsleeved smock devoid of pockets. The capsule hypothesis, therefore, could not be reasonably maintained unless it were determined where the containers were hidden before and after the red fluid appeared. Also, I had observed her hands so closely, and from so many different angles, that the palming procedure appeared highly unlikely.

"The cotton phenomenon would also be difficult to ascribe to legerdemain. Sison would have had to "palm" a piece of cotton after it appeared to enter the body. To produce the red streak on the cotton, which I noted after it had appeared to emerge from my abdomen, Sison would have had either to substitute cotton or break a capsule of red fluid on the same piece of cotton after it seemed to emerge from the skin. And what about the time when I appeared to see the cotton protrude from my flesh even when Sison was not touching it? This could have only been explained in terms of a hypnotic effect, and I simply did not feel that anyone was overtly or covertly making an attempt to alter my perceptions of the external world."

Dr. Hans Naegeli-Osjord

An M.D., psychiatrist and psychoanalyst, Dr. Naegeli, of Zurich, Switzerland, has spent a total of four months during six trips to the Philippines since 1971 studying psychic surgery. He was president of the Swiss Society for Parapsychology at the time he participated in the Meek-McCausland research in 1973. In addition to the following explanation of psychic surgery and related phenomena which Naegeli sent to us, interesting accounts of his and other researchers' experiences with non-medical cures—some quite dramatic—and paranormal abilities can be found in Alfred B. Stelter's superb book Psi Healing.

Since psychic surgery in the Philippines came to the knowledge of Westerners, many books and papers have been written, pro and con.

All those misunderstanding the phenomena and trying to explain them as sleight-of-hand—in my opinion—did not observe them in a neutral way, and most of them did not stay longer than two weeks, observing only a few of the healers. It is repeated, unannounced visits to observe many healers in a variety of situations that is convincing.

For to explain the phenomena, you have to let go all the scientific laws accepted by the followers of Galileo Galilei. The phenomena are not to be understood without a firm cognition (understanding) of *magic*. Magic means the fact that thinking and even perceiving in a very intense way may have an analogous effect on the materia. But that happens only if quite a lot of conditions are fulfilled.

Of course, magic has no ethical value in itself. It can be used as black and as white magic, the latter one by a good healer.

This healer ought to have highly mediumistic qualities, which means he must be a very good psychic. In addition, he has to be religious without any doubt and his intellect should not be prevalent or too much developed, as by so many Westerners. By long exercises as hermits and by fasting, they train themselves to use trance, self-hypnosis, and the faculty of mystic union (unio mystica), the "Satari" in Buddhism or "Samadhi" of the yogis. This mystic union happens with one of their "spirit guides" (archangel St. Michael, St. Paul and so on). They believe that this is the source of their power.

In psychic surgery, we meet all the phenomena parapsychology is dealing with, such as materialization, dematerialization, apports and psychoplastic (the psychical effect on the materia). We know the patterns through nuclear physics, where materia is transferred to energy and vice versa.

So, all phenomena to be observed in psychic surgery are not wonders, but extremely rare natural happenings. They belong to the fourth dimension of materia, not depending on space and time.

Most of the instant healing can't be explained without the acceptance of the human *subtle body* (etheric body, astral body), which is involved first and then acts on the material body.

All these facts mentioned lead to theories. The book by Marti and Don Sladek tells us the reality. It tells us how it is all going on in a very human manner and from minute to minute. This is most important for judging the phenomena and in the real sense is *complementary* to theories.

In my opinion it is an important fact that Marti is a psychic, too. So the healers feel at home and are not disturbed by a constant criticism, which generally destroys all psychic phenomena. The healers feel confident and at ease, so they can work in a favorable ambience. I know that some Westerners totally destroy the atmosphere with their criticism. But too much criticism is equally a sign of mental debility as no criticism!

This is to be stated for any scientist confronted with phenomena not mentioned in his schoolbooks of natural science.

Dr. Naegeli also reports the following documented cures by Philippine Healers for two of the cases in which he was directly involved:

Mr. K.D., 46 years old, from Switzerland had suffered extensive *psoriasis* since 1951 and was being treated with cortico-steroids. As a result, he had *necrosis* at the head of the femur (deterioration of the top of the thigh bone), general *osteoporosis* (breakdown of calcium in the bones), *chondropathy* (pain) in both knees and *discopathy* (pain in the spinal discs). Despite several conventional operations, K.D. had been in a wheelchair since 1969. In March 1972 Tony Agpaoa performed several "bloody operations" (psychic surgery). Subsequently, all functions were recovered including complete erection of the vertabral column. By 1976 he was able to walk for four hours in the mountains and the psoriasis was 90% gone.

Dr. W.F., 56 years old, dentist, M.D., a personal friend

of mine. In 1974 three rotator muscles were torn at the top of the arm in a skiing accident. In 1975 X-rays showed *capsula articularis humeri* (ligaments) torn. Surgeons stated there was no possibility of helping him and declared him a 30% invalid. In February 1976 he had a five minute session by Juanito Flores with spiritual injections, magnetic healing and adjusting movements, but no "bloody operation." *Restitutio ad integrum* took place in one treatment. As of November 1976: totally cured, normal power in the muscles, all movement restored.

Henry Rucker

The Reverend Henry E. Rucker is National Director of the Psychic Research Foundation and Chairman of the Board of the Essence of Hermetic Light Church, both in Chicago. He is a psychic diagnostician, working with Dr. Norman Shealey, M.D. at St. Francis Hospital and the Pain Rehabilitation Institute, La Crosse, Wisconsin; Rucker has participated in research in parapsychology at several private organizations, in addition to conducting classes on psychic phenomena at colleges, universities and institutes across the U.S. and in Africa. He wrote a syndicated newspaper column, guests frequently on talk shows, and has been a subject of dozens of articles and books. A noted healer, palmist, and dream analyst, Rucker became acquainted with Tony Agpaoa while Tony was visiting the United States. (They were introduced by Chicagoan Greta Diehl, who had just returned from the Philippines, where Tony performed a successful operation on her to remove a brain tumor.) Rucker decided to accept Tony's invitation to see for himself if psychic surgery was real. Ironically, the area in which he spent a month traveling with and observing many Healers was very near where he had been stationed in the Army. Among the Healers he met were Tony, Marcello, Terte, Josefina and Blance and the late Gonzales. Rucker's story:

Although I had a back problem (not serious) at the time my wife and I went to the Philippines, it did not occur to me that I would personally experience psychic surgery, but I did. Josefina Sison worked on my back and, to my and my wife's alarm, left some cotton in my back. I was afraid it might cause infection, but she removed it in a subsequent operation a couple of days later.

At the time I was there, the Espiritista was holding a sort of spiritual reunion or revival, and many of the Igarots, a Philippine mountain tribe, were coming down to the lowlands for healing, bringing bananas, papayas and mangos for fees. Occasionally a healer would collect a peso or two; that was all they were getting in payment for working on these people, practically nothing!

I moved in with Tony, lived in his house, and traveled around between Baugio and Manila. I watched Tony, and I watched Terte, and I watched Josefina do operation on operation on operation. I watched and I took pictures with my little Kodak Instamatic. (It wasn't a high-speed, but it was the best I had.) And I was satisfied, and I am today, that not only are the operations legitimate, but I really saw what I saw. I saw them go into the body, and contrary to the opinions of scientists and doctors, to my eyes the body was opened, and I saw parts come out, I saw intestines, I saw eyes, I saw teeth being extracted, I saw tumors being extracted, and from my viewpoint I did not see anything I could classify as fraudulent. Subsequently, I heard about the frauds. I don't know about the sleight-of-hand. I never did experience it. This was in 1968, and I don't mean they have changed since then; I don't know if they were doing it then. But I personally never saw anything I could say was a fraud. I watched them do magnetic healing, which sometimes was just as effective as psychic surgery. I watched the water turn to different colors. I watched Tony cut ten layers of adhesive tape with his tongue, I watched him do it with his finger, and I was astounded, yet I don't believe I was duped. And it seems an intelligent person will remember what he saw, and the camera, I believe, would not lie. If I was being hypnotized, certainly my camera was not being hypnotized!

So, I am one who is willing to go on record to say psychic surgery is a reality. I don't know how it works. I would never dare to say it works with separation of the body, or dematerialization, or anything like that, because I don't know. I only know what I saw. I'm not in a position to scientifically describe the phenomena. I don't know that many people would care if I did. I've heard explanations of it, but I've never been satisfied with the explanations of psychic surgery. I just don't know what happens. I only know that it does happen.

Dr. Harry Rich

The following is excerpted from a letter dated July 5, 1976 to Don and myself from Dr. Harry Rich, D.D.S., B.D.S. of Sydney, Australia. We began corresponding with Dr. Rich after Don read a story in an Australian newspaper about his experiences with the Philippine Healers.

I did indeed visit Baguio City in November 1974 in conjunction with giving some lectures at the University of the Phillipines Dental School in Manila. In Baguio I met and observed Placido Palitayan at work and I found him to be an earnest, quiet and apparently sincere man. He permitted me to watch him while he was performing several "operations" and at the same time photographs were taken by a professional newspaper photographer attached to the "Daily Mirror," a Sydney newspaper. I also met a lady journalist by the name of Leigh Bonheur who acted as leader of the group visiting Placido from Sydney for the purpose of being healed. Miss Bonheur herself had a large—what appeared to be—goitre in her neck, which was previously attended to by Placido and which, according to her account, had been reduced in size by his operations.

After watching Placido at work and after having some work done by him on my own body, I made a statement about my impressions to Miss Bonheur. I stated that I was unclear as to how he did the operations with the associated flow of blood and removal of various types of tissue. I also said that I was unclear as to how it came about that some of the patients obtained obvious relief from their symptoms. I made it clear that I saw no obvious acts of trickery and magic as practiced by stage magicians.

In short, I stated that I saw the work and that I was not clear as to how it was done and how he achieved the results which were quite often beneficial. In my own case, I felt symptomatically improved for quite some time.

At this stage I can only repeat what I have written above, to anyone wanting my opinion about psychic surgery. I saw it done, I don't know how it's done, I don't know how it works but it works in quite a sizable number of cases.

The Meek-McCausland Report

The Meek-McCausland group, working individually and in small teams, was well into a five-year worldwide study of spiritual healing when they came together in the Philippines just a few months prior to our trip. Some had researched psychic surgery before; some had not. After several weeks of observation and participation, all but two of the eleven members signed a public release of their findings on March 2, 1973. It is carefully worded because—according to recent communications we've had with Meek—while all nine agreed that materialization phenomena were involved, there was a difference of opinion as to whether the body is actually opened during psychic surgery. The document is written to avoid stating flatly that the body is open so they could concur in it as to the nature of the phenomenon at that time. Meek thinks that he and some of the others might not sign the same statement today, due primarily to increased instances of fraud in the past few years. Nonetheless, at least Drs. Naegeli, Stelter and Seutemann, following still more intensive research, (we have not been in touch with the remaining members of the group) still believe in the reality of the psi phenomena per se, as do many other qualified observers and patients who have gotten results.

Report of International Study Group
On Psychokinetic Phenomena
Related to Philippine Spiritual Healers

During our visit(s) to or stay in the Philippines, we, the undersigned, have, alone and in small groups observed the activities of several healers.

Each of us, reporting only as an individual and

not on behalf of any organization with which we may be connected, hereby confirms that psychokinetic phenomena which we observed during the healing activity:

1. Did not involve fraud,
2. Utilized no anaesthesia,
3. Did not use scalpel, razor blades or other instruments to open the body,
4. Required usually from 1 to 10 minutes to perform,
5. Permitted in most cases the healer and patient to remain in street clothes with no special precautions to maintain sterile conditions,
6. Appeared to cause little if any discomfort to the patient,
7. Left the patient without operative shock.

It is not within the scope of this initial study to assess the effectiveness of the Spiritual healing. Any such evaluation would require a considerable amount of time for detailed study and evaluation of the patient prior to and for a prolonged period after the healing. (NOTE: Two of the undersigned are of the opinion that they themselves underwent successful spiritual healing in prior visits to the Philippines. Their experiences are reported separately.)

It is our opinion individually that no one theory or combination of theories as yet considered, can, at this stage of study, adequately provide any acceptable scientific explanation of these phenomena which we observed.

Joaquin Cunanan Philippines	Retired Certified Public Accountant, President-General of Union Spiritista Cristiana de Filipinas, Inc. and President, Philippine Yoga Society, Inc.
Prof. B. Kirchgassner West Germany	Engineer, Fachhochschule, Ravensburg
Marcus McCausland United Kingdom	Health for the New Age Ltd., London Technical Advisor, National Federation of Spiritual Healers, London
George Meek United States	Engineer and psychic researcher, Life Energies Research, Inc., New York
Dr. H. Naegeli Switzerland	M.D., President, Swiss Parapsychological Society
Prof. Dr. Schiebeler West Germany	Physicist, Fachhochschule Ravensburg
Dr. Alfred Stelter West Germany	Nuclear chemist, physicist, parapsychology instructor
Dr. Sigrun Seutemann West Germany	Medical Practitioner
Donald Westerbeke United States	Biochemist, business executive, San Francisco

Dr. Lee Pulos, Ph. D.

Lee Pulos, Ph.D. is a clinical psychologist in private practice. His career has ranged from a traditional hypnosis practice to his current interests in holistic health and the collecting of cross-cultural data on paranormal healing and trance states. He has held teaching appointments at the universities of Indiana, Wisconsin and British Columbia, and is a Diplomate in clinical psychology. In addition to his extensive academic and clinical background, he is a "down-to-earth" pragmatist and is the co-owner/operations director of a large, successful business corporation. Since 1975 he has been listed in **Who's Who In The West.** *We had been told of his extensive independent research into several forms of paranormal healing, including psychic surgery in the Philippines. When we contacted Dr. Pulos, he graciously consented to comment on our book in conjunction with his own experiences and findings in the Philippines. Here is his statement:*

Marti Sladek has written an engrossing, honest and very perceptive account of her experiences among the psychic surgeons of the Philippines. Having been to the Philippines on two different occasions—witnessing and 'assisting' on over one thousand operations—I found her descriptions of the individualized techniques of the various healers to correspond almost identically to what I saw and experienced personally.

There is no doubt in my mind of the validity of the phenomena of psychic surgery—instances of faking notwithstanding. What the Sladeks have described is going to result in many people questioning and perhaps re-defining their world view. My own

Philippine experiences led to the eventual breaking of my 'cultural trance' and cognitive attachment to a three-dimensional linear but limiting perception of reality.

The most appealing aspect of her book was the warm yet objective presentation of her experiences without the cluttering of paranoid speculations or half-baked theories. Their approach throughout is —here is the evidence as we saw it and let the readers make up their own minds.

Implicit in the book of course is the element of magic—the real magic of consciousness permeating the universe. Through a variety of trance states, the. healers have found pathways of transcending ordinary restraints and working with and being at one with nature.

As with the Philippine healers, the history of Shamanism, Kahuna priests, North American Indian medicine men and African witch doctors is also characterized by dematerializations, laying on of hands, absent healing, hexings and materialization of matter from a healee's body. There are also cultural correspondences in the claims that most healing takes place at the level of the etheric or 'real' body rather than the dense body. The healing practises described by the Sladeks are not confined to the Philippines but can be witnessed daily in Brazil, Mexico, parts of the southern United States, Russia, and Africa. While the various locales differ in their metaphor to account for the healing energy, the 'magic' and process is basically similar in allowing one to transform his/her consciousness and enter into a harmonious partnership with nature.

I recommend that this book be set aside after the first reading. Think about the implications of the magic it describes and then read it again. One cannot help but end up looking beyond the ordinary perimeters of his/her being.

John Newcombe

Most tennis buffs would agree that John Newcombe is one of the great tennis players of all time: number one ranked in the world three times, Wimbledon singles champ three times (1967, 1970, 1971) and doubles winner six times, U.S. title holder twice (1967, 1973), World Tennis Cup crown in 1974 and Australian champion 1973-1975. Injury-plagued for the past few years, Newcombe—along with several other world class athletes from Australia—turned to the psychic surgeons for relief from tennis-related ailments. Not long after our return from the Philippines, we began reading in the newspapers that some pro tennis players had been treated by the Philippine Healers, among them such big names as Ray Ruffles, Tony Roche, Phil Dent and John Newcombe. We were, of course, very curious as to whom they had seen, what they'd had done, indeed if the wire service reports were totally accurate. But we had no idea how to reach any of them. Dr. Rich told us that Newcombe had described his experience on Australian TV, which made us more determined to find out how to get in touch with him. All we knew was that he had a U.S. base somewhere in Texas; we could go no further with it. As a last resort, in a move we never would have made had we known the tremendous pressure he was under at the time, we cabled him at Wimbledon, England right in the middle of the 1976 Wimbledon Tournament. A long shot, and we weren't overly confident that he'd even get it, let alone reply. But reply he did, anxious to read the manuscript and more than happy to share his and his colleagues' experiences with us. And a bonus—Newcombe's own "editorial comment" about our favorite word, "coincidence!"

It was a great pleasure to read the manuscript of the book on the psychic surgeons by Marti Sladek. I have been observed and treated by the healer Juan Blance. My experiences were almost identical with those described by the Sladeks. In 1973 I observed some operations, and in 1974 I had successful work done on a tennis elbow. I say successful because the swelling and soreness disappeared after the operation. It was not mental! In 1975 I returned for treatment on a knee injury. Blance manipulated and made an incision. He said the knee would get better, but it didn't. Four weeks later I was operated on in Texas to remove my cartilage.

Other tennis players having successful operations for long-incurred injuries are Ray Keldie and Phil Dent, who went to Blance for treatment of foot injuries, and Tony Roche and Ray Ruffles for treatment of arm and foot injuries from Placido. Karen Krantzcke, who went to Blance for treatment of her wrist injury in April of 1976, said she saw him fake the operation and was most upset. She then visited Placido and was very happy with his work.

In 1973 I was accompanied in my visit by a close friend who is a highly skilled surgeon in the U.S. He observed Blance closely and thought he was just a super magician, but could not explain the cutting. Blance used the doctor's hands several times and there was *definitely* no razor blade involved. I feel it is a hard lump for doctors to swallow that perhaps there is some truth in psychic surgery.

I myself believe there is something happening that modern medicine has skipped over during the centuries. I am not a believer in the supernatural and I believe in coincidence. I believe that through the centuries man will develop the ability to go *within* himself for healing, not just mentally, but physically. We are very primitive in our knowledge of what we are capable of.

In summary I would like to say I feel the book is an excellent report of what to expect from the Filipino psychic surgeons. It is interesting to note that Lance and Pam Mesh who are mentioned in the book as patients are very good friends of mine and were the first to tell me about the healers. (Coincidence???)

This book printed & bound for
Doma Press
by
The Lakeside Press
R.R. Donnelley & Sons Company